ARE YOU SMARTER THAN A
BABY BOOMER?
QUIZ BOOK

Gordon Kerr worked in the wine industry, bookselling and publishing before becoming a full-time author. He is the author of a number of books including *A Short History of the Vietnam War*, *Dead Famous* and *Great British Losers*. He divides his time between Dorset and Southwest France.

ARE YOU SMARTER THAN A
BABY BOOMER?
QUIZ BOOK

Edited by
Gordon Kerr

PALAZZO

This edition first published in the UK in 2018 by
PALAZZO EDITIONS LTD
15 Church Road
London SW14 9HE
www.palazzoeditions.com

Text, design and layout © 2018 Palazzo Editions Ltd

ISBN: 9781786750686
Printed and bound in Great Britain by CPI.

CONTENTS

INTRODUCTION

The past is, indeed a foreign country, as the writer, L.P. Hartley, sagely noted in his novel *The Go-Between*. When many of the so-called "Baby Boomers" came into the world, it was still reeling from the six or seven years of carnage wrought by the Second World War. The horrors of that time, unimaginable to us in Britain today, were fresh in the minds of people the world over and, indeed, the shockwaves were still being felt. Many British cities were devastated and children in urban environments amused themselves by playing on bomb-sites. The global economy was in a parlous state and in Britain the financial impact of the war was grievous. There were still severe shortages of essentials and rationing of foodstuffs, clothing soap and fuel, amongst other things, remained in place long after the conclusion of the war. The remaining restrictions on meat and other food finally ended in July 1954, a full nine years after the wild celebrations of V.E Day. This was the world into which some of the Baby Boomer generation were born, as indeed, the hangover from the war continued for some time.

The Baby Boomer generation is reckoned by most to consist of those born between 1946, when there was a post-war boom in childbirth, and 1964. But even though these people are grouped under one heading, there was, of course, a great disparity in the lifestyles of those born in the 1940s and 50s and those who grew up in the 1960s and 70s. The young people of the late 40s and 50s grew up in straitened circumstances as their country fought to rebuild itself. Only in the 1960s could it be said that we finally emerged from the clouds of war. Improving economies and a consumer boom gave the young people of this period a lifestyle of which previous generations could only dream. Not only was there the possibility of having a refrigerator and a television, increased spending on healthcare – and the NHS in Britain – also contributed to making this the healthiest and fittest generation ever.

Education, too, was available to all – in the West, at any rate. In Britain, the 1944 Education Act brought sweeping changes in the provision and organisation of education in England and Wales, with similar acts being passed for Scotland and Northern Ireland. The act increased opportunities for girls and the working class in general to access secondary education. It became the duty of the local education authority to provide school meals and free milk for pupils. Importantly, the school leaving age was raised from 14 to 15.

In 1951, the General Certificate of Education (GCE) was introduced, replacing the School Certificate and Higher School Certificate which had been the measure of a schoolchild's education since 1918. The GCE lasted until 1986 when it was replaced by the General Certificate of Secondary Education (GCSE). Many of the questions in this book are taken from GCE Ordinary Level papers.

One notion that is relentlessly rolled out every August when the exam results are published is that exams were more difficult back in the early years of the Baby Boomers' lives. Newspaper reporters seize the opportunity to file some easy copy at that time of year claiming this to be the case, often without much research being carried out as to whether it is really true. In fact, at this point, perhaps the second part of L.P. Harley's quote about the past should be wheeled out as it seems appropriate. The full text reads "The past is a foreign country; they do things differently there." And it does indeed seem that they did things differently six or seven decades ago, and that may be the biggest difference in education then and now. From the study of exam papers, it seems that questions were much more verbose. There was certainly no such thing as multiple choice, or if there was, it was extremely rare. Interestingly, the same style of question appears in exam paper after exam paper. It might be a question about ratios, or a question about percentages but the questions year after year are invariably very similar. They often deal in the same materials, Italian silk being one surprising topic, arising often in questions in which students were being tested on their ability to convert metres into yards. This was a useful skill given our trade with Europe at the time and a growing conviction that Britain should undergo metrication as suggested by the Hodgson Committee Report of 1949 which unanimously recommended compulsory metrication and currency decimalization within ten years. (Please note: we have changed some of the Arithmetic currency questions to decimals).

The repetition of question styles suggests, as is often said of education in the past, a greater degree of rote-learning. As a method of educating children rote-learning is still used in a number countries in Asia and the Far East, but nowadays, as a teaching method, it has become somewhat devalued and is heavily criticized by academics. This question repetition would, therefore, suggest entirely different teaching methods as well as different exam styles. Teachers could be fairly certain that certain questions would inevitably appear in the exam paper. Of course, when comparing eras it could be said that when Millennials were being examined, they were also being tested on a curriculum they had to follow. Therefore, the broad area to be examined was a known quantity, but questions were undoubtedly more varied in style and content. It could also be argued, however, that as a teacher works to the same curriculum year after year, he or she should become more familiar with its intricacies and better able to teach it as the years pass. This may also be true of examiners who will have settled into their role and the quality of the examination they provide should become more consistent, allow for fewer mistakes, and, indeed, become more predictable. That may be the equivalent nowadays to the knowledge in the 1940s and 50s of what question was going to be asked. It is interesting to see the comments of one teacher regarding the curriculum, or syllabus, then and now, "The thing to remember is that 40 or 50 years ago, the syllabus was about two pages long. Today the content is about 20 pages. What we have sacrificed in the move from O levels to GCSEs is depth for breadth."

It should also be noted that the content of exam questions six decades ago also left something to be desired. Questions were often poorly worded, badly laid out or even vague, rendering them difficult to answer. The language sometimes used might even have made it difficult for a child to understand a question. Our resident boffin, who provided many of the answers to the questions in this book, came across a number that were ambiguous or just impossible to understand.

Of course, when people claim that exams were harder back then, they are peering through rose-tinted spectacles. It is only human nature to do so. In reality, however, it is probable that most older people have little memory of their schooling, let alone the type of questions they might have faced in O Level English or in the Eleven-Plus. Nonetheless, some studies do confirm that exams used to be harder, most notably one by Loughborough University with its report entitled *Fifty years of A-Level mathematics: Have standards changed?* It seemed to confirm that Maths exams were indeed more difficult decades ago. But, significantly, it also found that standards had remained constant in the last twenty years.

Of course, there is one thing that the journalist, hunting for a few easy column inches, and the grumpy old man, or woman, searching for yet another rod to use to beat the youth of today, might be ignoring. Perhaps – horror of horrors! – young people are simply getting cleverer. In the measurement of IQ, the Flynn Effect is a term that was coined to describe the gradual improvement in IQ scores over time. One 2009 study, Raven's Progressive Matrices test, found that the average scores of British children in their tests rose by 14 IQ points from 1942 to 2008. A similar phenomenon was discovered by the Royal Society of Chemistry which undertook the Five Decade Challenge in 2008 in which 1,300 children sat tests taken from the numerical and analytical components of O level and GCSE exams over the past half century. Performance against each decade's exam questions rose as the decades came closer to the year of the initiative. The average score for questions from the nineteen-sixties was 15% and this rose to 35% for current (2008) examination questions. Interestingly, this study showed a huge leap in results from around the time the GCSEs were introduced in 1988. Since their introduction, scores have remained fairly stable.

It could be argued that young people today have more knowledge of the world and that this must have an effect on their general intellect. They mature years earlier than their equivalents of sixty or seventy years ago. They travel the world, or the world comes to them via the media, whether that be television, the cinema, the internet or from social media. Perhaps this makes a comparison of intellectual performance in exam conditions invidious, comparing apples with oranges, as it were. The needs and attitudes of young people now are vastly different to what they were before the invention of the teenager and the advent of music, fashion and entertainment created purely for them.

Despite this, it is fascinating to put yourself into the shoes of that post-war schoolchild and have a go at the type of exam questions he or she was faced with when those immortal and fairly terrifying words were uttered, as they are to this day, "You may turn over your paper and begin." *Are You Smarter than a Baby Boomer?* gives you the opportunity to answer genuine exam questions across a range of subjects from that era. Find out for yourself if post-war kids had it harder.

(By the way, if you enjoy pitting your wits against the Baby Boomer generation, why not do the same against the Millennials with *Are You Smarter than a Millennial?* featuring questions from SATs, 11+ and GCSE exam papers from the 1980s, 90s and noughties?)

QUESTIONS

ARITHMETIC

EXAM 1

1. Lucy goes to a Holiday Club every weekday for five weeks during the holidays. She pays £0.60 each time she goes. How much does she pay in total during the holiday?

2. Yvonne spends x pounds each day on her lunch at school. She spends y pounds each week on a bus pass to get her to and from school.
   How much does Yvonne spend altogether in 6 weeks? Which one of the following equations represents her actual expenditure?
   A. $30y + 30x$
   B. $6x + 6y$
   C. $30y + 6x$
   D. $6y + 42x$
   E. $30x + 6y$

3. Mrs Whiting bought 144 "lucky bags" for the Brownies' Christmas party. They come packed in boxes of 16. How many boxes of 'lucky bags' did Mrs Whiting buy?

Answers on page 125

4. In a local sweet shop there are 360 boxes of Belgian chocolates. 48 are given away as prizes in a special Valentine's prize draw. 192 are sold to the public at £4.60 a box.

How many boxes remain unsold?

5. Alexander's grandma is 5 times as old as Alexander was 3 years ago.

If Alexander's grandma is 60, how old is Alexander?

6. Mr and Mrs Fitzgerald take their 3 children to a special pop concert at a theme park. Tickets cost £7.00 each for adults. The price of a child's ticket is half that of an adult's.

How much does it cost the family to visit the theme park?

7. Roger places weights totalling 425g on an electric scale. He needs to make a total of 5.5 kilograms.

Which two of the weights below should he choose to make up the weight to the correct amount?

    A. 625g.

    B. 750g.

    C. 650g.

    D. 400g.

    E. 500g.

8. This half-term, Martin has taken seven times tables tests.
Here are his results out of 10:

8   5   9   4   6   4   8

What was his median score?

9. The ratio of flour to sugar in a cake is 7:4.
If 200g of sugar was used to make the cake,
how much flour was used?

10. Smoked salmon crisps cost 47p per packet.
Sophie bought 5 packets for herself and her friends.
How much change would Sophie get from a
£5 note.

EXAM 2

1. There are 12 sticks of 'Minty Fresh' chewing gum in a pack. How many packs could you make from 216 sticks of gum?

2. The local book shop has a sale. Every item in the shop is reduced by 25%. Melanie buys a set of encyclopaedias. The set normally costs £30.
   How much does Melanie have to pay for the books in the sale?

3. In the same book shop Melanie's little brother, Robert, bought a picture book for £1.50.
   What was the price of the picture book BEFORE the sale started?

4. How many faces has an octagonal prism?

5. A box contains 2 blue pencils, 3 green pencils and 4 red pencils.
   If I pick a pencil from the box at random (with my eyes shut), what is the probability that I will pick out a green one?
   - A. $\frac{2}{7}$
   - B. $\frac{1}{2}$
   - C. $\frac{1}{3}$
   - D. $\frac{1}{4}$
   - E. $\frac{2}{5}$

6. Look at the Venn diagram below. It shows how many children in Mrs Thompson's class like chocolate, ice cream or both. 2 children like neither. There are 32 children in the class.

If 26 children like chocolate and 20 like ice cream:

    (i) How many children like chocolate but not ice cream?

    (ii) How many children like only one flavour?

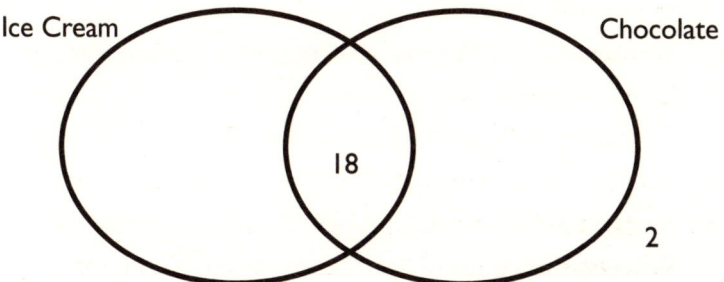

7. Find the missing number so that the equation balances.
$8 \times 9 - 16 = 7 \times 5 + ?$

8. Which one of the following numbers has factors of 2, 5 and 6?

20   35   40   55   60

9. What fraction of an hour is 12 minutes?

10. A runner did 4 laps of a track which was 400 metres in length in the morning, and double that distance in the afternoon.
How far did he run altogether?

EXAM 3

1. How many half-dozens are there in 22 + 12 + 8?

2. A man worked in his garden from 8.30 in the morning until 12.30, and then from 1.45 to 5.15.
   For how many minutes was he working there?

3. Tom weighs 40 kilograms and 200 grams. His sister is half as much again in weight.
   How much do they weigh together?

4. A boy had a sum to do – it was 17 x 13. By mistake, he multiplied 17 by 11.
   How far wrong was he?

5. A boy walked one-third of the distance between two places, 21 km apart, in 2 hours 14 mins.
   How long will it take him to walk, at the same rate, the remainder of the distance?

6. A bottle of lemonade and two buns cost 10p. If I had bought a bottle of lemonade and four buns, it would have cost me 14p.
   How much did I have to pay for the lemonade?

7. A schoolgirl went away on her summer holidays on July 25th and came back on August 21st.
How many complete days of these two months did the girl spend at home?

8. Some nuts are divided into equal piles, and each pile is divided into three equal smaller piles.
What is the smallest number of nuts with which you can do this?

9. A girl had 72p. She gave half of her money away to her brother, and a quarter of the remainder to her mother.
How much did she keep for herself?

10. If six men can do a job of work in 11 days, how long will three men take, working at the same rate?

EXAM 4

1. How many times does 9 go into 144?

2. Multiply $11\frac{1}{2}$ by 6.

3. A child at school has a quarter of a litre of milk per day. How many children are there in a class if 3 litres are taken one day at break?

4. The side of a square is 50 cm. How far is the distance all round in metres.

5. 7 books cost £2.10. What will 3 cost at the same rate?

6. I leave home at 8.13 a.m. I walk for 5 minutes, and then wait 2 minutes for my bus. It takes 27 minutes for the bus to reach school. How many minutes early am I if school does not start until 9 a.m.?

7. What is twice a quarter of 7?

8. 5 bobbelinks are equal in weight to 3 snooks. Which is heavier, a snook or a bobbelink?

9. Six years ago my sister was six years old. What will be her age in six years' time?

10. Which is the better buy: 5 apples at 7p or 7 similar apples at 10p?

EXAM 5

1. How many tiles 10 cm square are needed to cover a square whose sides measure 30 cm?

2. How many pence is half of £1 and a fifth of £1?

3. What is the total cost of 12 articles at 9½ p each?

4. A farmer owns three fields. In the first he has 24 cows, in the second double that number, and in the third double the number in the second. How many cows does he own altogether?

5. Three and a half times a number is 7. What is half of the number.

6. A man bought 425 plants at 20p per 100.
What did they cost him?

7. On a farm are 4 rabbits, 2 cats, 5 dogs, and 22 sheep. How many legs altogether do these animals have?

8. A man weighs 81 kilograms. His son is exactly half his father's weight. What is the weight of the son?

9. A boy owns 24 books. His friend has 16. How many must the first boy give to the second so that they have an equal number of books?

10. A map is drawn to a scale of 2 cm to 5 km. How far on the map is the distance between two towns 18 km apart?

EXAM 6

1. The average weight of p boys is q lb. The total weight of x of these boys is y lb.
   What is the average weight of the rest?

2. In a certain class examination the ratio of the passes to the failures was 13:5. If two candidates more had passed the ratio would then have been 7:2.
   How many failed?

3. A farm of 221 acres includes 60 acres of marshland, the rest being divided between grassland and arable land in the ratio of 5:2.
   If 7 acres of marsh are turned into grassland, while 10 acres of grassland are ploughed for use as arable land, find in its lowest terms, the new ratio of grassland to arable land.

4. A car travels 170 miles from London to Exeter at an average speed of 20 miles per hour, and returns at an average speed of 30 miles per hour.
   Calculate the average speed over the whole journey.

5. Two similar solids have heights of 6 centimetres and 9 centimetres respectively.
   Given that the volume of the smaller solid is 88 cubic centimetres, calculate the volume of the larger solid.

6. Find the quantity, in litres of ink, required to fill 750 rectangular ink pots each 2.5 centimetres long, 2.5 centimetres wide and 2 centimetres deep.

7. The average weight of the 8 tallest boys in a class was 50.25 kilograms and the average weight of the remaining 16 was 45.15 kilograms.
Find the average weight of all the boys in the class.

8. Working 8 hours a day at the same average rate, 45 men could do a job in 12 days. If they only work 7½ hours a day and the job must be done in 9 days, find how many men should be employed.

9. A tennis court 78 feet long and 36 feet wide is to be surrounded by a rectangular fence of wire-netting 9 feet high, erected 6 feet away from each long side and 10 feet away from each short side.
If the wire-netting is sold only in complete rolls 10 yards long and four feet 6 inches wide, find the number of rolls which should be bought.

10. The sum of the ages of two brothers, Peter and John, is 20 years 6 months. When Peter was half his present age he was 5 years older than John is now.
Find out how old Peter will be when John is 20 years of age.

EXAM 7

1. In a cake recipe, the ratio of flour to fat is 4:3. How much fat will there be in a cake containing 14 oz flour?

2. The eighteenth term of an arithmetical progression is double the twelfth term and the sum of these two is 9. Find the first term and the common difference.

3. A man of height 6 feet is walking along a horizontal plane towards a vertical lamp standard. At a certain point his shadow cast by the lamp is 20 feet long. When he has walked 6 feet more towards the standard his shadow is 16 feet long.
   Calculate the height of the lamp standard and find how long his shadow will be when he has walked a further 4 feet towards the standard.

4. A family having been on holiday for $14\frac{1}{2}$ days discovers on returning that a tap has been left dripping. To find how much water has been wasted, it is observed that the tap drips 7 times in 5 seconds, and that a jar of capacity 9 cubic inches is filled in 10 minutes. Find
   - (a) the volume of a drop, in cubic inches correct to two significant figures
   - (b) the number of gallons wasted, to the nearest whole number.
   [1 cubic foot = $6\frac{1}{4}$ gallons]

5. The average of three numbers is 58.
The average of two of them is 49.
Find the third number.

6. A man borrows £875, agreeing to pay interest at 4 per
cent per annum. After one year he pays the lender £90,
partly to pay the interest due for that year, and partly to
reduce the debt. He makes a similar payment of £90 at the
end of the second year. What debt is outstanding after the
second payment?

7. A cyclist pedals steadily along a road at a speed of 10 miles
per hour. The diameter of his rear wheel is 28 inches. If the
chain-driven wheel fitted to the rear wheel has 18 teeth
and the number of teeth on the wheel to which the pedals
are attached is 45, find the number of revolutions which
the pedals make per minute.
$[\pi = {}^{22}\!/_7]$

8. A baker wishes to make up 112 lb. of a mixture according
to the following recipe:

8 oz. flour

1 teaspoonful ($\frac{1}{4}$ oz.) baking powder

3 eggs

5 oz. castor sugar

4 oz. margarine

Assuming that an egg weighs 2 oz. find to the nearest
pound the necessary weights of flour, sugar and margarine.
Find also, to the nearest ounce, the weight of baking
powder required.

9. An aeroplane undertakes a flight of 2,350 miles in three
stages. It averages 300 miles per hour over the first stage
which is 960 miles. The second stage takes 2 hours 15
minutes at an average speed of 280 miles per hour.
If the journey is completed in a total flying time of
9 hours 15 minutes, what was the average speed for
the third stage of the journey?

10. The first term of an arithmetical progression is 16 and
the sixth term is 83.
Find the third term and the sum of the first 40 terms.

EXAM 8

1. A sum of money invested at $3\frac{1}{2}$% Simple Interest amounts after 4 years to £513.
Find the sum invested.

2. If the average length of my stride is 2 feet 9 inches, find the number of strides I take in walking quarter of a mile.

3. Two girls, Ann and Beryl, with one cycle between them, wished to go on a journey of 14 miles starting together. Ann cycled x miles at 8 miles per hour, left her bicycle and walked the rest of the way at 3 miles per hour. Beryl walked the x miles at 4 miles per hour and then cycled the rest of the way at 9 miles per hour.
If Beryl arrived 20 minutes ahead of Ann, find x.

4. A lighthouse A is 4 miles due N. of a lighthouse B. The bearings of A and B from a ship at C are 30° W. of N. and 60° W. of S. respectively.
Calculate the distances AC and BC.

5. The total wages bill in one year for a factory is £425,000, of which 20 per cent is paid for overtime work and the remainder for normal work. Payment for normal work is made to executives, skilled workers, and unskilled workers in the proportion $10 : 17 : 7$.

   (a) Calculate the wages bill for each class of worker for normal work.
   (b) The factory's full complement of workers totals 360 in the proportion $1 : 10 : 7$ for the three groups given above. The distribution of overtime pay between the three groups is in the proportion $0 : 9 : 8$. Calculate, correct to the nearest £, the average overtime pay for an unskilled worker in this year.

6. In one hour, a man can drive 35 miles further than he can walk. If he walks at x miles per hour, obtain expressions for the number of minutes taken to
   (i) drive one mile
   (ii) walk one mile
   (iii) If it takes him $10\frac{1}{2}$ minutes longer to walk than to drive one mile, find the speed at which he drives

7. Find 7 percent of £155.

8. Find the simple interest on £150 for 5 months at $2\frac{1}{2}$ per cent per annum to the nearest 1p.

9. A wholesaler sold three consignments of goods which were to retail at £80, £64 and £102. His retail customers were allowed discounts of 15 per cent, 10 per cent and 12½ per cent respectively.
Calculate the wholesaler's total receipts for these goods.

10. In a certain county borough during 1951, there were 1,376 live births of which 724 were male babies. 478 of all live births were classified as 'fair-haired', the rest being classified as 'dark-haired'.
If there were 184 'fair-haired' males, calculate, correct to two places of decimals, the ratio of 'fair-haired' females to 'dark-haired' females.

EXAM 9

1. An athlete ran a half-mile on ten occasions, his times being:
   2 min. 4 sec.; 2 min. 8 sec.; 2 min. 1 sec.; 2 min. 9 sec.;
   2 min. 14 sec.; 1 min. 59 sec.; 2 min. 7 sec.; 2 min. 12 sec.;
   2 min. 5 sec.; and 2 min. 3 sec.
   Determine for these times
   - (i) the mean
   - (ii) the median
   - (iii) the standard deviation

2. A square field whose perimeter is 0.75 miles is
   sold for £2,250.
   Find the cost per acre.

3. Solve the quadratic equation $5 - 3x - x^2 = 0$, giving
   your answers correct to three significant figures.

4. A piece of wire 20 inches long is to be bent to form a
   rectangle of area 22.75 square inches.
   Find the length of the rectangle.

5. Two men A and B form a business partnership with capitals of £1,500 and £3,500 respectively. They agree that each shall receive as a first charge on the profits an interest of 4% per annum on his capital. They also agree that A shall receive a management salary as a second charge on the profits and that the remaining profits shall be divided in the ratio of the capitals.

If the profits for one year amount to £1,150 and if B's total share is £525, calculate the amount which A receives as management salary.

6. Water is flowing through a cylindrical pipe, internal diameter 1.6 inches, into a cylindrical tank, internal diameter 2 feet. If the rate of flow of the water is 3.8 miles per hour, the tank is filled in 3 minutes. Find the internal height of the tank, correct to the nearest inch.

7. In 1960, the average number of cars produced each month for the first six months was 133,002. The number of cars produced in July was 94,054. What was the monthly average for the first seven months?

8. The following numbers give the mean hours of sunshine per day each month during the period January to August 1961:

1.4   2.3   4.9   3.3   6.8   7.3   5.3   5.5

Calculate the arithmetic mean and the standard deviation of these numbers.

9. Four different coins are tossed.
What is the probability that three or four heads are obtained?

10. The following information concerns the deliveries of all types of motor vehicles with two or three wheels during the three months April-June 1961.
In April, the total number of vehicles delivered was 16,970 which were valued at £2,104,000. Of these 3,020 vehicles were for export.
In May, the total number of vehicles fell by 630 and the total value was £1,817,000. Compared with the April figure, 690 fewer vehicles were exported.
In June, although the number of vehicles delivered for export was reduced to 2,000, the number delivered to the home market was 15,480. The total value of the deliveries fell by £54,000 compared with the corresponding value for May.
Tabulate the information suitably, giving for each of the three months mentioned the following information:

    (a) The total number of vehicles delivered.
    (b) The number of vehicles delivered to the home market
    (c) The number of vehicles delivered for export
    (d) The total value of the vehicles delivered.

EXAM 10

1. A rectangular tank of length 4 feet and breadth 2 feet contains water to a depth of 3 feet.
   If 37½ gallons of water are removed from the tank, find the depth of the water which remains.
   [1 cubic foot = 6¼ gallons]

2. A cube of lead of side 10 inches is melted down. Part of the lead is made into a cube of side 7 inches and the remainder into a sphere.
   Find the radius of the sphere in inches to one place of decimals.
   [The volume of a sphere of radius r = (⁴⁄₃)πr3.
   Take π = 3.142]

3. A motorcyclist started at 2pm on a journey from Oxford to Cambridge, a distance of 80 miles, riding at a speed of 24 miles per hour. After travelling 20 miles he had a puncture which took 40 minutes to mend. He then continued his journey at a speed of 20 miles per hour. At 5pm a car left Cambridge travelling to Oxford at 30 miles per hour.
   (i) Find graphically, or otherwise, the time and the distance from Cambridge when they met and the average speed of the motorcycle for the whole journey.
   (ii) Find also the times when they were 20 miles apart.
   [Take 1 inch to represent 1 hour and 1 inch to represent 10 miles]

4. A boy A runs 100 yards in x seconds and a boy B runs 1 yard in y seconds. B takes ⅕ second longer than A to run 100 yards. When B is given 3 yards start in a 100 yards race, he takes 1/10 second less than A.

    (i) Find x and y.

    (ii) Find also how many yards start B should be given in a 100 yard race in order that A and B should finish together.

5. A ball of string contains 88 yards. What length will be left after tying 86 parcels, each requiring 2 ft. 9 ins. of string?

6. Add together: 0.6, 3.025, 1.365 and from the total take away 3.275.

7. In order to reach his office by 9 a.m. a man leaves his house at 8.15 a.m. and cycles at the rate of 10 miles an hour.

    (a) What is the distance in miles from his house to the office?

    (b) If his bicycle breaks down after he has cycled for 40 minutes, find the number of yards and feet he must walk to get to his office.

8. A box holds 5.25 kilogrammes of oranges of average weight 75 grams. How many oranges are there in the box?

9. Express in knots a speed of 570 miles per hour, given that 1 knot is 6,080 feet per hour.

10. A red lamp flashes every 6 seconds, a green one every 8 seconds and a white one every 10 seconds.
If they all start flashing at the same instant, find:

   (a) the interval of time before red and white again flash together.
   (b) how many times, counting the first, red, green and white flash simultaneously in one hour.

Answers on page 130

EXAM 11

1. A man bought 6 of the articles A at £10 each and sold them at a profit of 30 per cent of the cost price. He also bought 8 of the articles B at £5 each and sold them so that he made a total profit of 34 per cent of his total outlay. Calculate the percentage profit on cost price at which he sold the articles B.

2. A room is 15 feet long, 10 feet wide and 8 feet high. The windows occupy altogether 42 square feet of wall space. The walls are to be painted, and one tin of paint covers 72 square feet.
   How many tins of paint should be bought?

3. A journey of 9 miles takes 33 minutes.
   Calculate the average speed in yards per second.

4. A hall 8 feet square is paved with 144 square tiles.
   How many of these tiles would be required to pave a rectangular hall 10 feet by 6 feet?

5. The average age of 3 boys and a girl is 12 years 7 months. If the average age of the boys is 12 years 10 months, find the age of the girl.

6. A car travelling across a city averages 28 miles per hour for the first 3½ miles. The next 1¼ miles through the shopping centre takes 12½ minutes, and the journey is then completed in a further 10 minutes at an average speed of 22½ miles per hour. Calculate

    (i) the time taken for the first 3½ miles

    (ii) the average speed for the whole journey

7. In a group of 600 people, 70 per cent are adults. If 110 of the children are girls, how many are boys?

8. Find the exact value of 32.548 ÷ 2.06.

9. Solve the equation
$$\frac{4p-1}{3} - \frac{3p-1}{2} = \frac{5-2p}{4}$$

10. When $x = 0$ the value of the expression $ax^2 + bx + c$ is −3. When $x = 3$ the value is 6, and when $x = -2$, the value is 11. Find a, b, c.

EXAM 12

1. Solve the simultaneous equations

(i) $x + y = 12$

(ii) $2x^2 + 3y^2 = 7xy$

2. Solve the equations

(i) $x^2 + 5x = 0$

(ii) $y^2 + 5y = 6$

3. Find x, given that

$5x - 4y = 2,$

$3y = 4x$

4. Solve the equation

$^x/_3 + {}^x/_2 = 2 - {}^x/_6$

5. Solve the equation

$x(x + 5) = 66$

6. Solve the equation

$(2x - 3)^2 = 13$

Give your answers correct to one place of decimals.

7. Solve the equation

$7x - 4x - 5 = 0$

8. Solve the equations

(i) $3x + 4y = 6$

(ii) $y = 2x + 7$

9. Solve the simultaneous equations

(i) $2x - y = 5$

(ii) $xy + 2 = 0$

10. Solve the simultaneous equations

(i) $x^2 + y^2 = 130$

(ii) $2y - x = 5$

EXAM 13

1. Find the value of
3.2 x 0.25 x 0.6125

2. Find the value of
$(x + 2) (x^2 - 2x + 4)$, when $x = 1$.

3. From the equation $3x - 0.7y = 13$, calculate y when $x = 27$.

4. A man's journey to town consists of p miles on his cycle at an average speed of v miles per hour followed immediately by 9p miles by car at an average speed of 3v miles per hour. Find an expression for the total time for his journey and express it as a simple fraction in its lowest terms.

5. In a triangle ABC, the sides AB and AC are equal, BC = 4 inches, and B = 70°.
Calculate AB.

6. Calculate the angle through which the minute hand of a clock rotates between noon and 12.26 p.m.

7. The Arctic Circle is a circle of latitude and its circumference is 9,900 miles.
Calculate the radius of the circle and its angle of latitude.
[Take the earth as a sphere of radius 3,960 miles and take π as $^{22}/_7$]

8. Find, correct to the nearest 1 inch, the length of the hypotenuse of a right-angled triangle whose other sides are 5 inches and 6 inches.

9. A rectangular room has length 17 feet 6 inches and breadth 12 feet. If the volume of the room is 2,205 cubic feet, what is its height?

10. A, B and C form a business with a total capital of £9,000. At the end of the year, their shares of the profits are £192.50, £231, and £269.50, respectively.
What amount of capital did each put into the business?

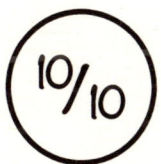

ENGLISH

EXAM I

1. Give the best single word to express the meaning of each of the following groups of words:

   (a) A ship which travels beneath the sea.

   (b) The outlying districts of a city.

   (c) The person who takes charge of a meeting.

   (d) Money or goods given to the poor.

   (e) A hash of meat and vegetables.

2. Rearrange the following phrases and clauses so that they make the best sense:

    (a) was pacing the deck
        the sound of oars
        when he heard
        Sir Robert Knowles
        early next morning
        the two sailors
        and there were
        returning to duty

    (b) which had been tied together
        and then he quickly
        he managed to free his hands
        unbound the rope round his ankles
        after a long time
        behind his back

3. What are the plurals of the following words?
    wolf
    echo
    footman
    axis
    boy's pencil

4. What are the past tenses of the following words?

> do
>
> go
>
> see
>
> build
>
> win

5. What are the names of the young of the following?

> duck
>
> cat
>
> swan
>
> rabbit
>
> cow

6. The plural of dog is dogs. What are the plurals of the following?

> monkey
>
> scissors
>
> knife
>
> goose
>
> mouse

Answers on page 132

7. From the words in brackets at the end of each sentence choose the correct one to fill in the blank spaces:

> (i) Choose …….. of the cards and return to the pack (either, any)
>
> (ii) …….. did he say the man was (who, whom)
>
> (iii) Neither of you …….. right. (are, is)
>
> (iv) Nobody in …….. senses could do such a thing. (their, his)

8. Form adjectives from the following:

> victory
>
> courage
>
> fortune
>
> success
>
> Spain

9. Give the plural of each of the following:

> child
>
> woman
>
> pony
>
> tooth
>
> fish
>
> brother
>
> sheep
>
> foot
>
> chief
>
> potato

10. Rewrite the following passage, putting in all the punctuation marks and capitals required:

a cat has not the same need for delicacies as a human being it can eat the black skin of filleted plaice it can eat bits of gristle that people leave on the side of their plates it can eat boiled cod

EXAM 2

1. Write one word to give the meaning of the following:

(a) Remaining in place and not moving.

(b) Without any limits.

(c) Deserving praise.

(d) Not able to make up his mind.

(e) To gather together.

2. Make the following pairs of sentences into one sentence by using one of the following words: *whose, who, whom, where.* A word or words may be left out and the order of the words may be changed:

(a) This is the place. We left the ball here.

(b) I went to visit my aunt Mar. She lives in the country.

(c) I gave the book to a boy. We saw the boy yesterday.

(d) Tom has two brothers. Their names are Dick and Harry.

(e) The girl ran for the doctor. The girl's father is ill.

Answers on page 133

3. Fill in the gaps in each of these lines:

   (a) A man who makes wheels for a cart is called a

   ……..

   (b) Cars are kept in ……..

   (c) The …….. make it easier now to find your way in the country.

   (d) At night sailors often steer by the ……..

   (e) Much land is wasted by the …….. which divide one field from another.

4. Rearrange these words, putting together in pairs the words that have a similar meaning:

far, seldom, order, mob, short, tramp, proud, old, cattle, stock, peak, wanderer, curt, top, rarely, command, conceited, crowd, distant, ancient

5. "Black" is the opposite of "white". Write the opposites of:

   absent

   broad

   guilty

   courage

   transparent

6. Write the following passage in the *present* tense, commencing 'The passengers take their seats...'

"The passengers took their seats and made themselves comfortable. Soon the train was full, and the guard looked at his watch. When he saw it was time to start, he blew the whistle, and waved his flag. The engine snorted and puffed, and the train began to move."

7. Put capital letters and punctuation marks in the following:

there replied mrs tinker flinging down the coin its only lords that care about farthings

8. What word is missing in each of the following sentences?
- (a) The money was safe and correct which proves the …….. of the treasurer.
- (b) …….. prevailed, in fact you could hear a pin drop.
- (c) The metal is expensive because it is ……..
- (d) After …….. his thirst he had a look at his wound.
- (e) The old man's hands swept over the …….. of the harp.

9. What is the masculine of each of the following?

cow

goose

mistress

vixen

empress

10. Give another word with a similar meaning to each of the following:

automobile

almanac

physician

quicksilver

radio

EXAM 3

1. The ten words that follow have been missed out of the poem. Put them in their proper places:

days, each, rainbow, bound, be, grow, heart, behold, began, die

My _____ leaps up when I _____,
A _____ in the sky:
So was it when my life _____;
So is it now I am a man;
So be it when I shall _____ old,
Or let me _____!
The Child is father of the Man;
And I could wish my _____ to be
_____ each to each by natural piety.

2. Arrange the following words in three columns under the headings:

Fishing   Farming   Building

harrow, tide, quay, mortar, trawler, eaves, harvest, rotation, maritime, silage, prefabricated, site, buoy, arable, vessel, girder, fertile, architect

3. What parts of speech are the words underlined:

    (a) <u>Slowly</u> <u>answered</u> Arthur from the barge.

    (b) Shall <u>I</u> meet other tired <u>wayfarers</u> tonight?

4. Underline the correct word of the two in brackets.

    (a) Neither of the men (was, were) able to go home.

    (b) (who whom) are you talking about?

    (c) He sent presents to you and (I, me).

    (d) My father could not (teach, learn) me.

    (e) They stayed (where, were) we left them with (there, their) friends.

5. The opposite of "hot" is "cold".
What are the opposites of:

    innocent

    wise

    strong

    future

    fertile

6. Fit the following *action words* into the blanks below:
pedal, climb, sail, mend, wheel, kindle, steer, push,
fly, wind

> You .... a puncture.
> You .... a barrow.
> You .... a boat.
> You .... a clock.
> You .... a kite.
> You .... a bicycle.
> You .... a pram.
> You .... a motor car.
> You .... a fire.
> You .... a tree.

7. Pick out the verbs and subjects in the following sentences:

> (a) The boy wheeled his bicycle along the pavement.
> (b) Only the contented enjoy true happiness.
> (c) Ask him for a match.
> (d) Down the street came a strange procession.
> (e) A company of soldiers, dressed in foreign
>   uniforms, stood round him.

8. Pair the animals in list (a) with the sounds they make from list (b).

List (a) horses, asses, wolves, lions, geese, hens, sheep, bees, cocks, cows.

List (b) cackle, roar, bray, neigh, bleat, howl, crow, low, hum, cluck

9. Give the missing word which is opposite in meaning to the word underlined:
  (a) Many <u>ancient</u> buildings are better built than ... ones.
  (b) After his long ... <u>freedom</u> was very welcome.
  (c) Instead of being <u>enriched</u> by his efforts, he found himself ...
  (d) Owing to his early <u>extravagance</u>, he was compelled to practice ...
  (e) Smoking was <u>permitted</u> in one room, but ... in the other.

10. Write one word in place of the following and note that the first letter of the word wanted is put there to help you:
  (a) Cannot be seen.   **i**
  (b) Easily broken into bits.   **b**
  (c) A person who dies for a cause.   **m**
  (d) A person who betrays.   **t**
  (e) One living all alone and wanting to be far from everybody.   **h**

EXAM 4

1. Change all the singular words in the following sentences into the plural and every verb into the past tense:

    (a) He tells his wife to bring her umbrella.

    (b) My cat catches the mouse easily.

    (c) That thief steals the farmer's goose after dark.

2. Give a single word for each of the following:

    (a) A place where plays are acted.

    (b) A number of people singing together.

    (c) A number of ships.

    (d) Goods carried by a ship.

    (e) Slightly wet.

    (f) A number of sheep.

    (g) A large number of herrings swimming together.

    (h) To get off a bicycle.

Answers on page 135

3. What do people use for the following purposes? Use *one* word only in each case.

Example: To keep a record of attendances – Register.

    (a) To find the day on which Christmas occurs.
    (b) To find the meanings of words.
    (c) To take sick or injured people to hospital.
    (d) To read and borrow books.
    (e) To keep a record of what happens each day.
    (f) To store a town's water supply.
    (g) To hold over their heads to protect them from rain.
    (h) To speak into when broadcasting.

4. "Girl" is the feminine of "boy". What is the feminine of the following:

    actor
    duke
    lion
    nephew
    bachelor

5. Form nouns by adding other nouns to each of the following:

> cow
> dog
> horse
> bird
> fish

6. What is the opposite of each of the following:

> hurt
> gentle
> proud
> advancing
> famous

7. The spaces in the following sentences show that words have been omitted. Replace the dashes by words chosen from this list:

its; it's; there; their; were; where

> (a) …….. you late this morning? Yes, we had a motor smash …….. the roads meet.
> (b) Has the river overflowed …….. banks? No! ……..
> not true.
> (c) …….. are five eggs in the nest.
> (d) The boys have picked …….. team for Saturday.

8. Correct where you think it necessary:

(a) I can't run no more.

(b) I won him playing marbles.

(c) Me and him helps to put up the shutters.

(d) Its not me that has broke the bulb.

(e) Being a fine night I have forgot my umbrella.

9. The following sentence is printed without capital letters, inverted commas, or punctuation marks. Rewrite the sentence correctly:

last Monday mary and I decided to go to newtown we went to market street and asked when the next bus went in about ten minutes said the conductor when does it return asked mary at six o'clock was the answer

10. Complete the following phrases:

As white as ……..

As black as ……..

As dead as ……..

As pure as ……..

As ugly as ……..

As straight as a ……..

As slippery as ……..

As happy as ……..

As dry as ……..

As poor as ……..

EXAM 5

1. Arrange these words in alphabetic order:
Albert, Ajax, Alfred, Austin, Anselm, Arthur, Asser, Alexander, Aidan, Anthony

2. Rewrite each of the following sentences using one word instead of those underlined:

   (a) The airman <u>came back</u> to his base.
   (b) The doctor said he was <u>full of hope</u>.
   (c) The bus stopped <u>all of a sudden</u>.
   (d) John <u>made up his mind</u> to work hard.
   (e) It <u>may be that</u> he has had an accident.

3. What special name do we give to people who sell the following:

   (a) Fish
   (b) Meat
   (c) Envelopes and newspapers
   (d) Pots, pans and nails
   (e) Sweets
   (f) Frocks and stockings
   (g) Cabbages and potatoes
   (h) Jackets, shirts and caps

Answers on page 136

4. Substitute a single word for the following phrases:

      (a) In a few words.

      (b) Without haste.

      (c) In a flash.

      (d) Not favouring either side.

5. Rewrite the following sentences in correct English:

      (a) Speaking as one who knows the district, Inverness, as a centre, is as good, if not better than Nairn.

      (b) Excuse me being late this morning; I am afraid I slept in.

      (c) I would have preferred to have seen you yesterday.

      (d) I was given the option of obeying him or to be dismissed; neither of the alternatives he offered were pleasant.

      (e) The patient seemed like to collapse, so we decided to send for the doctor.

      (f) These kind of road accidents are to be ascribed to the carelessness both of the drivers and pedestrians.

6. Correct, with the addition of all the proper marks of punctuation, the following passage:

i shall come to morrow Sunday afternoon and i ll bring a bible and shakespeares tempest with me I want to read the two passages that have most impressed me in my weeks reading the concluding chapters of the book of job the thirty-eighth to the end and praosperos speech to Ferdinand in act 4 scene I beginning you do look my son in a moved sort as if you were dismayed by cheerful sir our revels now are ended

7. Put the following passage of direct speech into indirect speech, prefixing some such phrase as "He said that…":

In all my experience of the flower shows in this village (and I can remember twenty-five) I have never seen a more magnificent display of blooms. There have been fifty more entries than last year; the membership of the Society has nearly doubled; and the funds, thanks to the care of the treasurer, are in a very satisfactory state. We can, therefore, expect that, good as this show is, next year's will be even better.

8. Name the figures of speech that appear in the following sentences:

    (a) They sank like lead in the mighty waters

    (b) I charge you by the law,
        Whereof you are a well-deserving pillar.

    (c) Sceptre and crown
        Must tumble down,
        And in the dust be equal made
        With the poor crooked scythe and spade.

    (d) Will all great Neptune's ocean wash this blood
        Clean from my hand? No; this my hand will rather
        The multitudinous seas incarnadine,
        Making the green one red.

    (e) The sons of Edward sleep in Abraham's bosom,
        And Anne my wife has bid the world good-night.

9. Form adjectives from:
verdure
character

10. Rewrite the following passage correctly, with the addition of all the proper marks of punctuation:
although it has long been a favourite among childrens books gullivers travels was originally written for adults its author jonathan swift was a great satirist perhaps the greatest in the history of English literature

EXAM 6

1. Give the meaning of each of the following phrases in one word:

    (a) Wishing evil to others

    (b) To pretend to be ill in order to avoid one's duties.

    (c) A composition in which an author's characteristics are ridiculed by exaggerated imitation.

    (d) Very ready to quarrel or fight.

    (e) An agreement obtained by mutual concession.

2. Explain the meaning of the following phrases:

    (a) To take a busman's holiday.

    (b) To run with the hare and hunt with the hounds.

    (c) To count one's chickens before they're hatched.

    (d) To cross the Rubicon.

    (e) To bell the cat.

3. Supply synonyms for the words italicised in the following passage:

Why do you *menace* me? I can *encounter* danger with *intrepidity* and I am not easily *daunted*, since I am not a *poltroon*.

4. Punctuate the following passage:

The blows on the door were repeated who knocks at this hour open and you will see I don't open to strangers

5. Form five words with the following prefixes:

(a) fore-
(b) un-
(c) in-
(d) co-
(e) ex-

6. Form five nouns with the following suffixes

(a) -ist
(b) -meter
(c) -phile
(d) -trix
(e) -latry

7. Write down a single word equivalent in meaning to the following groups of words.

(a) tear up by the roots

(b) living both on land and in water

(c) a universal remedy

(d) speaking two languages

(e) one who undergoes death or suffering for any great cause

(f) period of isolation imposed on voyagers

8. Complete each of the following idiomatic expressions by means of a suitable preposition.

(a) to be oblivious

(b) to be deficient

(c) to dissent

(d) to be different

(e) to hanker

9. Write down a noun which is formed from each of the following verbs:

    (a) embark

    (b) collide

    (c) emerge

    (d) magnify

    (e) prescribe

    (f) pretend

    (g) improvise

    (h) divert

10. Write out the following passage, properly arranged and punctuated, with capitals where necessary:

the salesman pointed out the advantages of the appliance its cleanliness its cheapness and its portability it can be yours for a payment of £5 on hire purchase he concluded how much a month would I have to pay I asked its for you to decide on the length of the period of payment mrs smith he replied

11. In the following sentences you are offered a choice of words. Rewrite each sentence using one of the words offered.

(a) It was childish / childlike of him to adopt such an attitude, and we were all annoyed by his peevishness.

(b) It was clear from my observance / observation that he was much affected / effected by the ceremony.

(c) They built the fortress high up on the mountain so that it would domineer / dominate the routes leading to the town, and the only way down from it to the valley was by a precipitous / precipitate path.

(d) He felt a momentous / momentary pang of regret, but he soon realized that he had done his best in the circumstances.

(e) He made a laudable / laudatory attempt to pass his rival, and we all congratulated him.

(f) He made a polite but concise / curt reply to my question.

Answers on page 140   71

12. By adding a prefix to the following words turn them into their opposites:

mobile
dutiful
harmonious
logical
trustful

13. What part of speech is each of the italicized words in the following sentences?

(a) He worked *hard* for his examination.

(b) The *sailor* gallantly took his place on the outside.

(c) Round the corner *came* a Tiger tank.

(d) You must either replace the money *or* resign.

(e) They looked forward to his *homecoming* very eagerly.

14. Punctuate the following passage, divide it into paragraphs, and supply capital letters:

will you do it hissed the villain giving his victims arm another twist oh screamed the victim if youll stop ill do what you want

EXAM 7

I. Write down the past tense of the verbs:

    occur
    lead
    pay
    try

2. Give the past participles of:

    excel
    speak
    reference
    benefit

3. Name the figure of speech contained in each of the following sentences:

(a) My life has crept so far on a broken wing.

(b) Or stain her honour or her new brocade
Or lose her heart or necklace at a ball.

(c) There were gentlemen and there were seamen in the navy of Charles the Second. But the seamen were not gentlemen, and the gentlemen were not seamen.

(d) … altar, sword, and pen,
Fireside, the heroic wealth of hall and bower
Have forfeited their ancient English dower
Of inward happiness.

(e) Close by the regal chair
Fell Thirst and Famine scowl
A baleful smile upon their baffled Guest.

(f) Nor dim and red, like God's own head,
The glorious sun purist.

4. Give words of opposite meaning to:

> established
>
> strange
>
> remote

5. Combine the following short sentences into a single sentence containing not more than two principal clauses:

> The clock struck twelve. I was startled. I had delayed too long. I resolved, nevertheless, to carry out my plan. I had prepared it with great care.

6. What single noun is used to describe a soldier who hires his services out for pay?

7. Rewrite the following passage correctly, adding all the necessary punctuation:

> across the road theres a big shop called Charles polytechnic stores ltd where they sell boys and mens clothes their goods are first class but many persons cant afford those high prices of theirs

8. Suggest

> (i) a single noun that means the story of one's own life written by oneself.
>
> (ii) a single adjective that means before the flood.

9. Rewrite the following passage in direct speech:

He told us that he had never doubted our courage. What he had heard that day, however, made him question the wisdom of our plan. He asked if we understood how eager and well trained our opponents were.

10. Form

(i) an adjective from credulity

(ii) a verb from facility

(iii) a noun from loquacious

11. Rewrite each of the following sentences, with the phrase in italics converted into a clause:

(i) *On his return home*, he had supper.

(ii) You must tell me *the reason for your lateness*.

(iii) *Despite his slowness* the tortoise beat the hare.

(iv) *Weather permitting*, we shall go to the seaside on Saturday.

(v) *With their usual efficiency* the Romans subdued the province.

12. Insert the correct prepositions in the following sentences:

   (i)   This is the very reverse……..that.

   (ii) This conduct is subversive……..discipline.

   (iii) A battle is different……..a siege.

   (iv) Have you no sympathy…….a deaf man?

   (v)   He tried to impress us……..his qualifications……..the post.

   (vi) Bodily exercise is conducive……..good health.

   (vii) He was……..variance……..his brother.

   (viii) We rely……..you entirely.

13. By adding the appropriate prefix, give the word which is exactly opposite in meaning to each of the following:

      similar

      noble

      legible

      rational

      friendly

14. Replace each of the following expressions by a single word equivalent in meaning:

(i) an instrument measuring the rise and fall in temperature

(ii) the science which studies plant life

(iii) a place where birds are kept

(iv) the statement of income and expenditure presented annually to Parliament

(v) an apparatus for hatching eggs

15. Form a verb from:

stimulus

sympathies

Form an adjective from:

community

muscles

GENERAL SCIENCE

1. Name the main substances that are excreted from the human body by each of the following:
(a) The kidneys
(b) The lungs
Name one other excreting organ and state one of its functions.

2. When the time is noon at Greenwich, state the local time at a point
(i) 30° due W. of Greenwich
(ii) 30° due N. of Greenwich

3. (i) Name two substances (other than water) transported in the blood of a human being.
(ii) State one function of the blood not connected with transport.

4. (i) What two substances are required for the production of carbohydrates in green plants?
(ii) What is the source of the energy used in converting these substances into carbohydrates?
(iii) Name one carbohydrate produced in this way?

Answers on page 145

5. Write down the chemical symbols for each of the following:

   (i) Oxygen

   (ii) Iron

   (iii) Copper

   (iv) Hydrogen

   (v) Silver

   (vi) Magnesium

6. What are the chemical and common names for the following?

   (i) $CaCO_3$

   (ii) H_2O

   (iii) NaCl

7. Where in a plant do the following processes take place?

   (i) osmosis

   (ii) diffusion

   (iii) evaporation

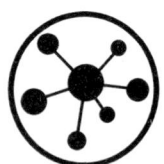

8. From the following list of substances:

brass

sulphur

air

calcium chloride

calcium oxide

sulphur dioxide

select

    (a) a base

    (b) a diliquescent substance

    (c) a non-metallic element

    (d) an alloy

9. Name

    (i) the largest body in the solar system

    (ii) two planets further from the sun than the earth

10. From the following list of metals:

zinc

steel

soft iron

aluminium

Select the most suitable to be used for

    (a) a compass needle

    (b) galvanising iron

    (c) electric conductor cables

Answers on page 145

11. State two factors that determine the amount of heat produced in the heating element of an electric fire.

12. Mention, in each case, one important natural phenomenon which depends on:
    (a) water on being cooled contracts until it reaches 4° centigrade, after which it expands
    (b) water expands on freezing

13. Give three examples of change in the physical or chemical state of solid substances brought about by the action of heat.

14. What temperature on the Centigrade scale is equivalent to 98.4° Fahrenheit?

15. Name one substance which would dissolve the first-named solid but not the second in each of the following mixtures:
    (a) zinc filings and copper filings
    (b) ammonium chloride and chalk
    (c) chalk and sand

16. Give the name of one substance which causes temporary hardness and one which causes permanent hardness of water.

17. State the law of multiple proportions.

18. Give the name (not the symbol) of

(a) a metal which readily burns in air

(b) a metal which displaces hydrogen from cold water

(c) a metal which displaces copper from a solution of copper sulphate

(d) a metal which burns spontaneously in chlorine

(e) a non-metal which readily burns in air

(f) a non-metal which displaces iodine from a solution of potassium iodide

19. Name one example in each case of a salt which on heating

(a) loses water of crystallization

(b) gives nitrogen

(c) gives a brown gas

20. A compound has the following percentage composition by weight: hydrogen 5%, nitrogen 35%, oxygen 60%.

(i) Calculate a formula for the compound.

(ii) What is the name of the compound, assuming it is a nitrate?

21. Give the names and chemical formulae of the following substances:

(a) limestone

(b) washing soda

(c) green vitriol

(d) slaked lime

22. Name four common soluble impurities which may occur in tap-water.

23. Give the name of a hydrocarbon which at the ordinary temperature is

(a) gaseous

(b) liquid

24. Give the chemical name of

(a) black lead

(b) red lead

(c) white lead

(d) litharge

25. Give the names of two elements commonly used as conductors of electricity.

26. (i) What are the constituents of mortar, other than water?

(ii) What chemical process is involved in the setting of mortar?

27. State Archimedes' principle.

28. What is meant by the calorific value of a fuel?

29. What is meant by the term dew point?

30. Define a watt.

What does it measure?

31. Name the materials used for the following purposes:

(i) The filament of an electric lamp

(ii) The element of an electric fire or heating coil.

(iii) Fuse wire

GENERAL INTELLIGENCE

TEST I

1. What relation to you is:

   (a) your brother's son.

   (b) your mother's sister.

   (c) your father's father.

   (d) your mother's mother.

   (e) your son's wife.

2. A chimney-sweep did the following six things:

    (a) looked to see if brush was showing from chimney.

    (b) was paid by Mrs. Smith.

    (c) booked an order to clean Mrs. Smith's chimney.

    (d) cleared up any mess on the floor.

    (e) brushed the chimney.

    (f) called at Mrs. Smith's house.

What is the correct order in which he did these six things?

3. Write down the answers to the following questions on numbers.

    (a) What is the third odd number above 21?
    (b) Add together all the even numbers between 3 and 13.
    (c) Write down the middle even number between 72 and 92.

4. Underline the two words in each pair of these brackets which make the same kind of pair as the two words at the beginning of each group:

(a) FORWARD, BACKWARD (slow, speed, quickly, slowly)

(b) ALWAYS, NEVER (sin, right, sinner, crime, wrong)

(c) ONE, FIRST (seven, seventeenth, seventieth, seventh)

(d) FOOT, FEET (part, toe, finger, party, toes)

(e) GARAGE, CAR (hay, horse, yard, shed, stable)

(f) TREE, OAK (beech, plant, giraffe, leaf, animal)

5. If there are more vowels than consonants in the word TOMATO, write down the word VEGETABLE; if the number of consonants is greater, write down the word FRUIT. If the number of vowels equals the number of consonants, write the plural of the word.

6. What is the longest word you can take out of the word INSTRUMENT where all the letters come next to each other?

7. Two brothers, Ted and Jim, were both born on January 1st.
Which of the following statements is correct?

    (a) They are twins.

    (b) They are not twins.

    (c) They may be twins.

8. Arrange the following words under these three headings:

FARMER   GROCER   TAILOR

pickles. sty. jams. twine. cotton. byre. tea. scissors.
orchard. soap. tape measure. trough.

9. In the passage below, a number of words are mixed up.
Write out the words correctly.

During the rwa, my aerfth was sent to Iltya where he was
in demcoanm of a greeitnm. One day, a German dserilo
was htcgua, and he turned out to be an cforeif.

10. Here are some arithmetic sums with the signs left out. Put
in the correct signs.

    (a) 3   5   11   = 19

    (b) 4   4   2   = 18

    (c) 7   12   7   = 12

    (d) 10   2   2   = 3

    (e) 6   10   6   = 2

11. Write down the five colours WHITE, RED, GREEN, BLACK, YELLOW as headings, and under each one put the following words according to their colours:

pillar box. banana. coal. flour. emerald. daffodil. ruby. salt. mustard. soot. lipstick. tar. grass. peas. snow.

12. If you had to write down the numbers from 81 to 89 inclusive, how many times would you have to write the figure 8?

13. Take the next odd number above 83 from the next odd number below 98.

14. In the following group of numbers, subtract the smallest even number from the largest odd one and find how many times your answer will divide into the largest even number.

44   52   16   13   8   8   7   20   21

15. (a) If my watch is five minutes fast, and the 8.45 bus for school is 5 minutes late, at what time by my watch does the bus leave?

(b) If my watch is 5 minutes slow, and it takes me twenty minutes to walk to school, what time will it be by my watch if I leave home so that I am at school by 8.45 right time?

16. Four numbers in each line below are similar in some way, but one number is out of place. Write down the number that is different from the others.

(a)   14.   35.   28.   43.   21.
(b)   4.   25.   35.   9.   16.
(c)   2.   6.   18.   53.   162.
(d)   15.   24.   31.   42.   51.
(e)   37.   53.   19.   43.   21.

17. Here are seven words which appear on the same page of a dictionary: HINDER. HILT. HILL. HINGE. HIGH. HIM. HIGHLY. Decide the right order in which they appear in the dictionary and write down the middle one.

18. The numbers below represent the letters in the name of a famous city in England.

1   2   3   4   5   6   7   8   9   10

Letters 6 and 9 are the same. 5 and 8 are your other vowels besides 2. 2, 3 and 4 make up the name of a busy little insect. The last four letters are also the name of a town in Lancashire, as well as meaning "to hide in the ground".
Write out under the numbers the corresponding letter, providing the name of the city.

19. Below are the jumbled names of ten flowers. Rearrange the letters in your mind to make the names, and then write down against each number the last letter of the flower.

1. OSRE	2. UITLIP	3. CCOSUR
4. NAPSY	5. YILL	6. RETSA
7. ADHILA	8. LOITEV	9. MENANEO
10. YAIDS		

20. (a) If in a code VXUDS stands for the word STRAP, what word does SDUXV stand for? How would you write SPRAT in the same code?

(b) In another code, B is written for C, A is written for B etc. Work out the answer to the following question.

NM VGZS CZX NE SGD VDDJ HR DZRSDQ LNMCZX?

21. In the following passage ten words have been left out. The missing words are:

accompany.	terrible.	another.	teacher.	because.
on.	wanted.	and.	ill.	his.

Write down the numbers 1 to 10, and against each number write the missing word.

Tom said that he ...1... to go home from school ...2...

he felt …3…. His …4… ordered …5… boy to …6… him
to …7… home. …8… the way they started to play in the
road, …9… there was a …10… accident.

22. In a code, letters are represented by numbers, as
D = 2, C = 3, A = 6, E = 0, and B = 4.
Answer the following:

(a) What number would you get by adding all the
letters together?

(b) Add B and C, multiply by D, and subtract A. How
many times is B contained in your answer?

(c) How many times will C go into the product of B
and A?

(d) What fraction is C added to D of B added to A?

(e) If I have D dozen, how many halves will that be?

(f) Write down the largest number that can be made
out of the figures for which the letters A, B, C, D
and E stand.

(g) If I divide B times C into D times A, and the
answer is F, what number would F be in the code?

23. By adding one letter, anywhere, to each of these groups of letters, you can make a real word. Put the real word in each case.

Example: STIK – STICK

MRRY
STRNGTH
WRON
TULP
HERT
FASK
LUGH
SPY

24. There are four girls whose names are Jane, Janet, Mary and Mabel.

Jane and Janet are short and fair.
Mary is dark, but not short
Mabel is short and dark.
Mary and Janet go to boarding school.
Mabel and Jane go to day school.

    (a) Which girl is short and goes to boarding school?
    (b) Which girl is tall and goes to boarding school?
    (c) Which fair girl goes to day school?
    (d) Who are short and not dark?

25. Each of the following sentences contains one extra word which ought not to be there. Put the sentence into its correct order and find the extra word. Write down the first letter of that word as your answer.

Example: HAS LEGS TAILS COW A FOUR – A COW HAS FOUR LEGS: Extra word TAILS – letter T

    (a) Isles England, Scotland are France British the in and,

    (b) six four eight make and four.

    (c) game a cricket is summer pitch.

    (d) going yesterday we where are?

    (e) comes tomorrow never why?

    (f) sail ships sailing sea the are to.

26. (a) Here is a group of five whole numbers; one is missing.

3   17   11   ...   18

Half of the missing number is double another. The missing number is not the largest in the group, nor is it an odd one. What is the number that is missing?

(b) Here is a group of five whole numbers; one is missing.

2   11   ...   1   5

All the numbers added together are twice the largest number. Complete this statement: The missing number is either ... or ... .

(c) Here is a group of four numbers; one is missing.

10.   4   ...   11

Two of the numbers in the group add up to the same total as the other two. The missing number is the largest in the group. What is the missing number?

27. Arthur was born 12 years ago, 5 years before Betty, who is 2 years older than Anne. Tom is half Arthur's age.

    (a) Who is the youngest

    (b) Who is the second-eldest?

    (c) In how many years' time will Tom be as old as Arthur is now?

28. (a) In this sentence: *The groom put the remaining ten ponies into their stables*, alter the word which tells you there were more than ten ponies to begin with.

    (b) In this sentence: *These difficult experiments were conducted by enthusiastic scientists*, alter the word which tells you that the scientists were interested in their work.

    (c) In this sentence: *We looked at our grimy faces in the glass; we were not surprised that Ponting did not recognize us*, alter the word which explains why Ponting did not recognize them.

    (d) In this sentence: *The Essex is a popular make of typewriter*, change the word which tells you that many people use an Essex to a word which means that the typewriter is of the newest kind.

29. (a) What relation is Mrs. Smith to her daughter's brother?

(b) What relation is Tony Brown to his father's father?

(c) What relation is Mr. Jones to his nephew's father, if Mr. Jones does not have a sister and is unmarried?

(d) What relation is Mary Robinson to her father's sister?

30. In each of the following lines, underline the two words which make the same kind of pair as the two words in brackets at the beginning of the line.

(YES, NO)   accept, hate, not, refuse, pleasure.

(HAT, HEAD)   top, glove, forehead, hair, hand.

(ARTIST, HEAD)   picture, carpenter, saw, seen, scene.

(NEAR, CLOSE)   far, dwell, dwelling, live, nearby.

(PALE, PALER)   paling, tree, good, water, better.

(THAMES, RIVER)   colour, London, Chelmsford, brown, stream.

(WE, US)   me, they, their, there, them.

TEST 2

1. Underline the longest and the shortest word in the sentence below:

READ EACH QUESTION CAREFULLY BEFORE YOU ANSWER IT

2. Find one letter that is contained in only three of the following words and then write down the word that does not contain that letter:

sail   number   lion   also

3. Arrange these objects according to some resemblance:

thrush   bus   cow   bee   bicycle   plane

4. Look for the differences between the numbers in each of these series and complete them:

(a) 1	2	3	4	....	....	....
(b) 4	8	16	8	4	....	....
(c) 1	2	4	8	16	....	....
(d) ½	....	1½	2	2½	....	....
(e) .05	.5	....	....	500	....	50,000

5. The person who stole Brown's purse was neither dark, nor tall, nor clean-shaven. The only persons in the room at the time were (a) Jones, who is short, dark and clean-shaven; (b) Smith, who is fair, short and bearded; (c) Grant, who is dark, but not clean-shaven.

Who stole Brown's purse?

6. A spy uses code to send his messages. He writes his message, then rewrites it, using for each letter the next letter in the alphabet. He then reverses the order of the words in the message, and the order of the letters in each word. Below is the result.

What does it mean?

EFIDUBX   FSB   FX   MVGFSBD   FC.

7. Look at this example:

beef   pork   mutton   cow

Three of the words are names of kinds of meat. The other word is the name of an animal. It has been underlined because it is different from the others.

Now go through the following examples, underlining the word in each row that you think is different from the other three.

Remember, just one word in each row.

(a)	hat	coat	dress	umbrella
(b)	tree	bush	shrub	wood
(c)	meat	pork	beef	lamb
(d)	water	milk	wine	bread
(e)	carpet	rug	sweeper	mat
(f)	bicycle	car	bus	lorry
(g)	rose	petal	daisy	foxglove
(h)	smoke	cigar	cigarette	pipe
(i)	polish	desk	table	chair
(j)	theatre	cathedral	chapel	church
(k)	apple	orange	lemonade	plum
(l)	geography	lesson	history	arithmetic
(m)	salt	pepper	mustard	sugar
(n)	good	bad	excellent	worthy
(o)	singing	working	dancing	idling

8. Each of the sentences given here can be made into better sense by interchanging two words. Draw lines under those words.

Example: Bones eat dogs.

Now do the sentences below for yourself. Remember, underline just two words in each sentence.

(a) Fred went into the bicycle on his town.
(b) The people soldiers as the cheered marched down the street.
(c) Tibby the mouse caught a cat.
(d) The children were beach on the running.
(e) Jane fell over the room as she ran round the stool.
(f) All the whistle stood still when the children blew.
(g) There are family boys and three girls in the two.
(h) Soldiers wear airmen clothes and khaki wear blue clothes.
(i) Jane made her cobbled slowly over the way road.
(j) The load horses dragged a black of corn to the barn.
(k) John park in the played.
(l) The people were so tea that they were glad to get a cup of tired.
(m) The kettle was hob merrily on the boiling.
(n) Katie with playing was her doll.

9. Choose the correct word with which these sentences should be ended.

Example: Man is to boy as woman is to GIRL.

(a) Country is to nation as home is to ....
(father, family, mother, house)

(b) War is to storm as peace is to ....
(dull, calm, wind, rain)

(c) Long is to short as good is to ....
(happy, bad, reward, tall)

(d) Bird is to air as fish is to ....
(chips, swimming, flying, water)

(e) Rifle is to bow as bullet is to ....
(spear, arrow, shield, quiver)

(f) Water is to jug as prisoner is to ....
(jail, judge, soldier, policeman)

(g) Fingers are to hand as toes are to ....
(head, knee, body, feet)

(h) Pencil is to drawing as knife is to ....
(tearing, carving, ripping, eating)

10. Correct these absurd sentences by crossing out ONLY what is incorrect. (Do not cross out too much, and do not add anything.)

The first boy to follow Jack across the brook who was the farmer's younger daughter.

Now by crossing out differently, you can leave another sensible sentence.

My two brothers all went to work at the same time.

11. If a pair of words mean nearly the same thing underline the letter S. If they are opposite underline O. If they are neither the same nor opposite, underline N.

(a) long	short	S	N	O
(b) excellent	perfect	S	N	O
(c) house	beef	S	N	O
(d) upper	lower	S	N	O
(e) sharp	acute	S	N	O
(f) bread	jam	S	N	O

12. Here is a question for you with answers printed after the question.

Example:

Jack is taller than Tom. Tom is taller than Mary

Who is the tallest?

TOM   MARY   <u>JACK</u>   ONE CANNOT TELL

The answer is JACK. We have underlined it.

Now do these. Underline the right answer. If your answer is ONE CANNOT TELL, underline it.

(a) Mary is fatter than John. Susan is fatter than Mary.
Who is the fattest?
JOHN   MARY   SUSAN   ONE CANNOT TELL

(b) Tim is shorter than Dick. Dick is shorter than Fred.
Who is the tallest?
TIM   DICK   FRED   ONE CANNOT TELL

(c) Mary has less money than Joan. Ann has less money than Joan.
Who has the least money?
MARY   JOAN   ANN   ONE CANNOT TELL

13. Three girls are sitting on a bench. Martha is on the right of Molly, and Mary is on the right of Martha.
Which girl is in the middle?

14. Here are some questions with answers underneath. Underline the right answer.

I walk 3 miles to the east, then 4 miles to the south, then 3 miles to the west.

(a) How far am I from my starting point?
I MILE 2 MILES 3 MILES 4 MILES ONE CANNOT TELL

(b) In which direction must I go to reach my starting point?
EAST WEST   NORTH SOUTH ONE CANNOT TELL

15. Write in the spaces the word or words which you think ought to be there:

(a) BOOTS are to ....
As GLOVES are to HANDS.
(b) For a HORSE a STABLE; for a COW a ....
(c) .... is to WRITING as
.... is to PAINTING.
(d) A SAILING-SHIP aground is like a
BIRD without ....

16. Put in the missing numbers and signs:

(a) 3 + 3 + 3 − 3 = ?
(b) 3 ? 3 ? 3 ? 3 = 81
(c) 3 x 3 + 3 + 3 = ?
(d) 3 ? 3 ? 3 ? 3 = 9

17. The last word in each sentence is missing. It has been hidden away among the four words given in brackets. Look at each sentence, find the missing word, and draw a line under it.

Example: Cat is to kitten as dog is to
(cow   hen   <u>puppy</u>   pig)

(a) Light is to dark as day is to
    (sky   stars   night   dull)
(b) Penny is to money a s cabbage is to
    (plant   beef   tree   bush)
(c) Cushion is to chair as mattress is to
    (large   sofa   bed   sleep)
(d) Button is to coat as garter is to
    (boot   foot   stocking   knee)
(e) Sit is to stand as smooth is to
    (soft   rough   edge   surface)
(f) Heavy is to light as large is to
    (small   big   edge   surface)

18. Underline the words in the brackets which give the right answer:

(a) To make far-off scenes appear near, sailors use (microscopes, stethoscopes, telescopes).

(b) A vault is (a kind of salt, something to do with electric light, a burial place).

(c) A chisel is (used to catch mice, a whistle, a tool).

(d) A goal is (a score at football, a prison, a funny word).

(e) Hake is (a fish, a steady thing, short for shake).

VERBAL REASONING

1. In each question below, one letter from the word on the left must be moved into the word on the right to make two new words. The letters must not be re-arranged. Both new words must make sense. Write the two new words in the space provided.

Example: CLIMB LOSE (C) LIMB CLOSE

(a). CHEAT WARS ……………………. …………………….

(b). PAINT BRAN ……………………. …………………….

(c). FIRST PAWN ……………………. …………………….

(d). CLOTH SORT ……………………. …………………….

(e). SPORT LACES ……………………. …………………….

(f). TRAMP PIER ……………………. …………………….

2. In each sentence below, one word, which is in capitals, has had three consecutive letters taken out. These three letters will make one correctly spelt word without changing the order. Write the three-letter word in the space provided.
Example: John bought a new COMER (PUT)
COMPUTER

(a). Jennifer ALS does her work very neatly

………………………..

(b). The lady ARGED the flowers in the vase

………………………..

(c). Jason took a MIE to tie his shoe laces

………………………..

(d). The PAING was hung on the wall

………………………..

(e). The porch light was GING in the dark

………………………..

(f). Grandma always wears her comfy SPERS in the house………………………..

3. In each question, find the number that will complete the sum correctly and write it in the space provided.

Example: 25 + 17 − 3 = 12 x 3 + (3)
(a). 15 x 4 + 24 = 58 + ( )
(b). 7 x 5 − 3 = 8 x 2 + ( )
(c). 70 ÷ 5 x 3 = 2 x 3 x ( )
(d). 45 + 18 = 9 x ( )
(e). 5 x 12 + 12 = 3 x 8 x ( )
(f). 50 x 7 − 100 = 100 ÷ 4 x ( )

4. In each question below, find two words, one from each group, that are the closest in meaning. Underline one word from each group.

Example (<u>sleep</u> run walk) (smile laugh <u>snooze</u>)

(a). (tread trod limp) (stiff tyre step)

(b). (smooth smother soothe) (rough ease raw)

(c). (manager mangle manual) (handbook handle handsome)

(d). (loan lone clone) (married engaged single)

(e). (increase diminish release) (decrease unease finish)

(f). (rotate relate relation) (resolute relaxed revolve)

5. A B C D E F G H I J K L M N O P Q R S T U V W X Y Z

The alphabet has been written above to help you answer the following questions.

In each question below, some of the words are in code. The first code word in each question has been worked out for you.

Now work out the second word in the question using the same code.

Example: If the code for TRAP is USBQ, what does DPME mean? Answer: COLD]

(a). If the code for BLAME is CNDQJ, what does TVHER mean? (_____)

(b). If the code for MEMORY is NCPKWS, what is the code for FORGET? (_____)

(c). If SZAKDR means TABLES, what does BGZHQR mean? (_____)

(d). If the code for RIGHT is QGFFS, what is the code for WRONG? (_____)

(e). If XRNQJ means SMILE, what does YFXYJ mean? (_____)

(f). If the code for TRUMPET is UUVPQHU, what is the code for CYMBALS ? (_____)

6. Read the following statement, then find the correct answer to the question and place a cross in the box next to the correct answer.

Jake, Hannah and Tanya each run in a timed cross-country race.

Tanya starts her run at 10.00 am. Hannah takes 5 minutes less than Jake to complete the course. Jake started his run 10 minutes before Tanya and finished at 10.20 am. Hannah finished at 10.15 am.

If these statements are true, which one of the sentences below is true?

A. Hannah runs faster than Tanya.

B. Jake and Tanya take the same amount of time.

C. Tanya is the last to finish.

D. Hannah and Jake started at the same time.

E. Jake finished after Tanya.

7. Read the following statement, then find the correct answer to the question and write it in the space provided.

Matthew is half as old as Zena will be next year. Simone is 6. Zena is two years older than Simone was last year.

How many years old is Matthew? (_____) years

8. In these questions, find the two words, one from each group that will complete the sentence in the best way. Underline one word from each group.

Example: Time is to (first, second, third)
as distance is to (gram, kilo, metre) <u>second,</u> <u>metre</u>

(a). 28 is to (January, February, March)
as 30 is to (June, July, August)

(b). Water is to (cold, liquid, drink)
as ice is to (frozen, clear, solid)

(c). Leaf is to (tree, plant, tea)
as bean is to (runner, broad, coffee)

(d). Navy is to (blue, sea, sailor)
as army is to (salvation, soldier, slave)

(e). Harp is to (pluck, angel, string)
as drum is to (strum, skin, stick)

(f). Rose is to (flower, rise, plant)
as sang is to (song, sing, tune)

9. Three of these four words are given in code.
The codes are not written in the same order as the words and one code is missing.

PALM LAST ROSE MEAT
8647 1458 5437

For the following questions, write the answers in the space provided.
(a). Find the code for the word METAL

(_____)

(b). Find the code for the word SMALLEST

(_____)

(c). Find the word for the code 7455637

(_____)

10. Three of these four words are given in code.

The codes are not written in the same order as the words and one code is missing.

POUR RUDE TYPE DATE
1653 9761 5423

For the following questions, write the answers in the space provided.

(a). Find the code for the word TRADER

(_____)

(b). Find the word for the code 21345

(_____)

(c). Find the word for the code 941453

(_____)

11. In the second half of the following sentences supply words opposite in meaning to those in bold type in the first half.
Example: The animals proved to be not wild and fierce but _____ and _____
Answer: but tame and gentle

a) Formerly the girl was a help to her mother, _____ she is a _____

b) Although the exterior of the building looked ugly, the _____ was quite _____

c) Metals expand when heated, but _____ when _____

d) The entrance to the cinema is very wide, but the _____ is rather _____

e) The hero was proud in the hour of victory, but the vanquished were _____ in the hour of _____

f) Wealth makes a man lazy, but _____ makes him _____

g) My friend's pearls are real and expensive, not _____ and _____

h) This evening, in the darkness, I lost my watch, but tomorrow, in _____ I hope to _____ it.

i) The young and the hopeful should remember the _____ and the _____

j) The Scriptures teach us to love truth and _____
Note: close synonyms will be acceptable in these answers

12. Rewrite the following sentences so as to show the actual words used by the speakers.

Example: Sentence given: He asked me who I was.
Answer: He asked me, 'Who are you?'

a) I called to him to stay where he was.

b) Gareth asked his teacher if he might have a new pencil.

c) Mary replied that she would be going home that night.

d) The boy was told that he and his friends were to return the next day.

13. The word required to complete each of the following sentences must be formed from the word printed in capitals alongside the sentence.

Example: BRING Food was _____ from a farmhouse.

Answer: brought

a) DISTURB Hooligans caused a _____ in the High Street.

b) BRUTE The brigands made a _____ attack on the travellers.

c) PERMISSION "_____ me to accompany you, Sir," said Mr. Micawber.

d) AGREE There was _____ among us not to touch each other's property.

e) INSTRUCT We were given our _____ and then dismissed.

f) DEMONSTRATION The conjuror prepared to _____ how the trick was done.

g) ORIGIN One must enter only _____ poems in the competition.

h) MAJESTY The great liner sailed _____ down the channel.

i) COWARD Long John Silver was guilty of many crimes but _____ was not one of them.

j) BREVITY The chairman made a _____ speech and sat down.

ANSWERS

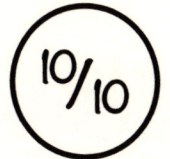

ANSWERS: ARITHMETIC

EXAM 1

1. £15
2. E
3. 9
4. 120
5. 15
6. £24.50
7. B and E
8. 6
9. 350g
10. £2.65

EXAM 2

1. 18
2. £22.50
3. £2.00
4. 10
5. ⅓
6. (i) 10; (ii) 14
7. 21
8. 60
9. ⅕
10. 4,800 metres

EXAM 3

1. 7
2. 450
3. 100 kilograms and 500 grams
4. 34
5. 4 hours 28 minutes
6. 6p
7. 34 days
8. 6
9. 2p
10. 22 days

EXAM 4

1. 16
2. 69
3. 12
4. 2 metres
5. 90p
6. 13 minutes
7. 3.5
8. snook
9. 18
10. 7 apples at 10p

EXAM 5

1. 9
2. 70
3. £1.14
4. 168
5. 1
6. 85p
7. 132
8. 40.5 kilograms
9. 4
10. 7.2 cm

EXAM 6

1. $(pq - xy) \div (p - x)$
2. 10
3. 2:1
4. 24 mph
5. 297 cubic centimetres
6. 9.375 litres
7. 46.85 kilograms
8. 58
9. 20
10. 33 years 6 months

EXAM 7

1. 10.5 oz
2. The first term is –2.5, the common difference is 0.5
3. The lamp is 15 feet high. When he has walked a further 4 feet his shadow will be 13 feet 4 inches
4. (a) 0.01 cubic inches; (b) 68 gallons
5. 76
6. £762.80
7. 48 revolutions
8. 39 lbs flour; 24 lbs sugar; 19 lbs margarine; 19 oz baking powder
9. 200 miles per hour
10. The third term is 42.8; the sum is 11092

EXAM 8

1. £450
2. 480 strides
3. $x = 8$
4. BC = 2 miles (to two decimal places); AC = 3.46 miles (to two decimal places)
5. (a) Executives: £100,000, Skilled workers: £170,000, Unskilled workers: £70,000; (b) £286
6. (i) $60 \div (x + 35)$; (ii) $60 \div x$; (iii) 40 miles per hour
7. £10.85
8. £1.56
9. £214.85
10. 0.82 : 1

EXAM 9

1. (i) 2 minutes 6.2 seconds; (ii) 2 minutes and 6 seconds;
   (iii) 4.73

2. £100

3. 1.193; -4.193

4. 3.5 inches x 6.5 inches

5. £200

6. 68 inches

7. 127,438

8. Mean = 4.6; Standard deviation = 2.096 to three decimal
   places)

9. $\frac{5}{16}$

10.

	Total No. of Vehicles Delivered	No. of Vehicles Delivered to the Home Market	No. of Vehicles Delivered for Export	Total Value of the Vehicles Delivered
April	16,970	13,950	3,020	2,104,000
May	16,340	14,010	2,330	1,817,000
June	17,480	15,480	2,000	1,763,000

EXAM 10

1. 2 feet 3 inches
2. 5.4 inches
3. (i) Time they meet = 5.36pm, Average speed of motorcycle = 22.86mph (to two decimal places); (ii) 5.12pm, 6pm
4. (i) $x = 9.8$, $y = \frac{1}{10}$; (ii) 2 yards
5. 27 feet 6 inches
6. 1.715
7. (a) 7.5 miles; (b) 1,466 yards 2 feet
8. 70
9. 495 knots
10. (a) 30; (b) 31

EXAM 11

1. 40%
2. 5
3. 8 yards per second
4. 135
5. 11 years 10 months
6. (i) 7.5 minutes; (ii) 17 miles per hour
7. 70
8. 15.8
9. $p = 1\frac{3}{4}$
10. $a = 2$; $b = -3$; $c = -3$

EXAM 12

1. (i) $x = 9, y = 3$; (ii) $x = 4, y = 8$
2. (i) $x = -5, 0$; (ii) $y = -6, 1$
3. $x = -6$
4. $x = 2$
5. $x = 6$
6. $x = 3.3$ or -0.3
7. $x = \frac{5}{3}$
8. (i) $x = -2$; (ii) $y = 3$
9. (i) $x = \frac{1}{2}, y = -4$; (ii) $x = 2, y = -1$
10. (i) $x = 9, y = 7$; (ii) $x = -11, y = -3$

EXAM 13

1. 0.49
2. 9
3. 97.14 (to two decimal places)
4. 4p/v hours
5. 5.85 inches
6. 156 degrees
7. 1575 miles; 66.56 degrees (to two decimal places)
8. 8 inches
9. 10 feet 6 inches
10. A - £2,500, B - £3,000, C - £3,500

ANSWERS: ENGLISH

EXAM I

1. (a) Submarine; (b) Suburbs; (c) Chairman/woman/person; (d) Charity; (e) Stew.

2. (a) Early next morning, Sir Robert Knowles was pacing the deck when he heard the sound of oars, and there were the two sailors returning to duty.; (b) After a long time, he managed to free his hands, which had been tied together behind his back, and then he quickly unbound the rope round his ankles.

3. wolves; echoes; footmen; axes; boys' pencils

4. did; went; saw; built; won

5. duckling; kitten; signet; kit; calf

6. monkeys; scissors; knives; geese; mice

7. (i) any; (ii) who; (iii) is; (iv) their

8. victorious; courageous; fortunate; successful; Spanish

9. children; women; ponies; teeth; fishes; brothers/brethren; sheep; feet; chiefs; potatoes

10. A cat has not the same need for delicacies as a human being. It can eat the black skin of filleted plaice; it can eat bits of gristle that people leave on the side of their plates; it can eat boiled cod.

EXAM 2

1. (a) stationary; (b) boundless, absolute, eternal; (c) laudable, commendable; (d) indecisive; (e) collect, amass, combine

2. (a) This is the place where we left the ball.; (b) I went to visit my aunt Mar who lives in the country.; (c) I gave the book to a boy who we saw yesterday.; (d) Tom has two brothers whose names are Dick and Harry.; (e) The girl whose father is ill ran for the doctor.

3. (a) wheelwright; (b) a garage; (c) maps; (d) stars; (e) hedges

4. order & command; seldom & rarely; old & ancient; mob & crowd; proud & conceited; peak & top; far & distant; short & curt; tramp & wanderer; cattle & stock

5. present; narrow; innocent; cowardice; opaque

6. "The passengers take their seats and make themselves comfortable. Soon the train is full, and the guard looks at his watch. When he sees it is time to start, he blows the whistle, and waves his flag. The engine snorts and puffs, and the train begins to move."

7. "There," replied Mrs Tinker, flinging down the coin. "It's only lords that care about farthings."

8. (a) honesty; (b) silence; (c) rare; (d) quenching; (e) strings

9. bull; gander; master; dog/fox/reynard; emperor

10. motorcar; calendar; doctor; mercury; wireless

EXAM 3

1. My heart leaps up when I behold
   A rainbow in the sky:
   So was it when my life began;
   So is it now I am a man;
   So be it when I shall grow old,
   Or let me die!
   The Child is father of the Man;
   And I could wish my days to be
   Bound each to each by natural piety.

2. Fishing: tide, quay, trawler, maritime, buoy, vessel; Farming: harrow, harvest, rotation, silage, arable, fertile; Building: mortar, eaves, prefabricated, site, girder, architect

3. (a) adverb & verb; (b) pronoun & noun

4. (a) was; (b) whom; (c) I; (d) teach; (e) where & their

5. guilty; foolish; weak; past; barren

6. You mend a puncture; You wheel a barrow; You sail a boat; You wind a clock; You fly a kite; You pedal a bicycle; You push a pram; You steer a motor car; You kindle a fire; You climb a tree.

7. (a) wheeled & boy; (b) enjoy & the contented; (c) ask & him; (d) down & procession; (e) stood & him

8. Horses & neigh; asses & bray; wolves & howl; lions & roar; geese & cackle; hens & cluck; sheep & bleat; bees & hum; cocks & crow; cows & low.

9. (a) modern; (b) incarceration; (c) impoverished; (d) frugality; (e) prohibited

10. (a) invisible; (b) brittle; (c) martyr; (d) traitor; (e) hermit

EXAM 4

1. (a) They told their wives to bring their umbrellas; (b) Our cats caught their mice easily; (c) Those thieves stole the farmers' geese after dark.

2. (a) theatre; (b) choir; (c) fleet; (d) cargo; (e) damp; (f) flock; (g) school; (h) dismount

3. (a) calendar; (b) dictionary; (c) ambulance; (d) library; (e) diary; (f) cistern; (g) umbrella; (h) microphone

4. actress; duchess; lioness; niece; spinster

5. cowshed; doghouse; horseshoe; birdbrain; fishfinger

6. healed; rough; humble; retreating; infamous

7. (a) Were you late this morning? Yes, we had a motor smash where the roads meet.

   (b) Has the river overflowed its banks? No! it's not true.

   (c) There are five eggs in the nest.

   (d) The boys have picked their team for Saturday.

8. (a) I can't run any more.

   (b) I beat him playing marbles.

   (c) He and I helped to put up the shutters.

   (d) It's not me that broke the bulb.

   (e) Being a fine night, I forgot my umbrella.

9. Last Monday, Mary and I decided to go to Newtown. We went to Market Street and asked when the next bus went. "In about ten minutes," said the conductor. "When does it return?" asked Mary.

   "At six o'clock," was the answer.

10. As white as a sheet/ghost; As black as coal/night; As dead as a doornail/dodo; As pure as the driven snow/snow; As ugly as sin; As straight as an arrow; As slippery as an eel/a fish;

As happy as a sandboy/Larry; As dry as dust/a bone; As poor as a church mouse

EXAM 5

1. Aidan, Ajax, Albert, Alexander, Alfred, Anselm, Anthony, Arthur, Asser, Austin

2. (a) The airman returned to his base.

   (b) The doctor said he was optimistic.

   (c) The bus stopped suddenly.

   (d) John resolved to work hard.

   (e) It's possible he has had an accident.

3. (a) Fishmonger; (b) Butcher; (c) Stationer; (d) Ironmonger; (e) Confectioner; (f) Hosier; (g) Grocer; (h) Outfitter

4. (a) concisely/briefly; (b) languidly/leisurely; (c) immediately/instantly; (d) neutral

5. (a) Speaking as one who knows the district, Inverness, as a centre, is as good as Nairn, if not better.

   (b) I'm sorry I was late this morning; I am afraid I slept in.

   (c) I would have preferred to see you yesterday.

   (d) I was given the option of obeying him or being dismissed; neither of the alternatives he offered were pleasant.

   (e) The patient seemed likely to collapse, so we decided to send for the doctor.

   (f) These kinds of road accidents are to be ascribed to the carelessness both of the drivers and pedestrians.

6. I shall come tomorrow, Sunday afternoon, and I'll bring a Bible and Shakespeare's *The Tempest* with me. I want to

read the two passages that have most impressed me in my weeks' reading: the concluding chapters of the Book of Job (the thirty-eighth to the end) and Prospero's speech to Ferdinand in Act 4, Scene 1, beginning, "You do look, my son, in a moved sort. As if you were dismayed. Be cheerful, sir. Our revels now are ended."

7. He said that in all his experience of the flower shows in the village (and he remembers twenty-five of them) he had never seen a more magnificent display of blooms. He added that there had been fifty more entries than last year; that the membership of the Society had nearly doubled; and that the funds, thanks to the care of the treasurer, were in a very satisfactory state. He therefore expected that, good as this show was, next year's would be even better.

8. (a) simile
   (b) metaphor
   (c) metonymy
   (d) hyperbole
   (e) understatement

9. verdant; characteristic

10. Although it has long been a favourite among children's books, "Gulliver's Travels" was originally written for adults. Its author, Jonathan Swift, was a great satirist: perhaps the greatest in the history of English literature.

EXAM 6

1. (a) Malevolence

(b) Malingering

(c) Parody

(d) Combative

(e) Compromise

2. (a) A holiday or form of recreation that involves doing the same thing that one does at work.

(b) To support or attempt to placate both sides of a conflict or dispute.

(c) One should not make plans that depend on something good happening before one knows that it has actually happened.

(d) Irrevocably commit to a course of action, make a fateful and final decision.

(e) To attempt, or agree to perform, an impossibly difficult task.

3. Why do you threaten me? I can meet danger with courage and I am not easily intimidated since I am not a coward.

4. The blows on the door were repeated. "Who knocks at this hour?"

"Open, and you will see."

"I don't open to strangers!"

5. (a) Foreground; foresight; forehead; forecastle; forecast; foretell; foreman etc.

(b) Unfair; unfairly; unfairness; unfelt; unseen; unfitting; unformed; unrest; unemployment etc.

(c) Inattention; indefensible; inexpensive; inorganic; invariable etc.

(d) Coadjutor; cohabit; cognate; cofounder; coproduction etc.

(e) exclude; except; exhibit; exit; exceed; exhale; exhaust; exterior etc.

6. (a) Apologist; dramatist; machinist; novelist; realist; socialist; fascist etc.

(b) Altimeter; barometer; perimeter; pentameter etc.

(c) Anglophile; bibliophile; demophile etc.

(d) Aviatrix; executrix; dominatrix; administratrix; inheritrix etc. No longer in common usage

(e) Idolatry; Mariolatry; bardolatry etc.

7. (a) uproot; pluck

(b) amphibious

(c) panacea

(d) bilingual

(e) martyr

(f) quarantine

8. (a) to be oblivious to

(b) to be deficient in

(c) to dissent from

(d) to be different to

(e) to hanker for

9. (a) embarkation
   (b) collision
   (c) emergence
   (d) magnification
   (e) prescription
   (f) pretence
   (g) improvisation
   (h) diversion

10. The salesman pointed out the advantages of the appliance: its cleanliness, its cheapness and its portability.
    "It can be yours for a payment of £5 on hire purchase," he concluded.
    "How much a month would I have to pay?" I asked.
    "It's for you to decide on the length of the period of payment, Mrs. Smith," he replied.

11. (a) childish
    (b) observation / affected
    (c) dominate / precipitous
    (d) momentary
    (e) laudable
    (f) concise

12. (a) immobile
    (b) undutiful
    (c) inharmonious
    (d) illogical
    (e) distrustful

13. (a) adverb

(b) noun

(c) verb

(d) conjunction

(e) noun

14. "Will you do it?" hissed the villain, giving his victim's arm another twist.

"Oh!" screamed the victim, "If you'll stop, I'll do what you want."

EXAM 7

1. occurred

led

paid

tried

2. excelled

spoke

referenced

benefited

3. (a) metaphor
(b) zeuma
(c) chiasmus
(d) metonymy
(e) personification
(f) litotes

4. temporary, unstable, indefinite, untrue or close synonyms
common, ordinary, familiar, standard or close synonyms
near, sociable, probably, warm or close synonyms

5. When the clock struck twelve, I was startled, feeling I had delayed too long, but I resolved, nevertheless, to carry out the plan I had prepared with such great care.

6. Mercenary

7. Across the road, there's a big shop called Charles' Polytechnic Stores Ltd where they sell boys' and men's clothes. Their goods are first class, but many people can't afford their high prices.

8. (i) autobiography
(ii) prediluvian

9. "I have never doubted your courage,' he said. 'What I have heard today, however, makes me question the wisdom of our plan. Do you understand how eager and well trained our opponents are?"

10. (i) credible

(ii) facilitate

(iii) loquaciousness (or loquiacity)

11. (i) When he returned home, he had supper.

(ii) You must tell me why you are late.

(iii) He ran slowly, but the tortoise beat the hare.

(iv) If the weather conditions are suitable, we shall go to the seaside on Saturday.

(v) The Romans acted with their usual efficiency and subdued the province.

12. (i) This is the very reverse of that.

(ii) This conduct is subversive to discipline.

(iii) A battle is different from a siege.

(iv) Have you no sympathy for a deaf man?

(v) He tried to impress us with his qualifications for the post.

(vi) Bodily exercise is conducive to good health.

(vii) He was at variance with his brother.

(viii) We rely on you entirely.

13. dissimilar

ignoble

illegible

irrational

unfriendly

14. thermometer

botany
aviary
budget
incubator

15. stimulate
sympathise
communal
muscular

ANSWERS: SCIENCE

1. (a) urea and uric acid; (b) carbon dioxide; The large intestine excretes faeces; the skin excretes excess water; the liver excretes bile

2. (i) 10 am; (ii) Noon

3. (i) correct answers include red blood cells, white blood cells, platelets and plasma, within which can be found hormones, waste substances such as carbon dioxide, and nutrients such as amino acids; (ii) 1) Protection: white blood cells, destroy invading microorganisms, antibodies fight disease and platelets help with blood clotting. 2) Regulation: blood helps regulate pH and hydration

4. (i) carbon dioxide and water; (ii) sunlight; (iii) correct answers include glucose, starch, cellulose or lignin

5. (i) O; (ii) Fe; (iii) Cu; (iv) H; (v) Ag; (vi) Mg

6. (i) calcium carbonate; (ii) water; (iii) sodium chloride

7. (i) in cells; (ii) in leaves; (iii) in stomata on leaves

8. (a) calcium oxide; (b) calcium chloride; (c) sulphur; (d) brass

9. (i) the Sun; (ii) Jupiter, Saturn, Uranus, Neptune

10. (a) steel; (b) zinc; (c) aluminium

11. Resistance and current

12. (a) cold water sinks, meaning that ecosystems can survive closer to the surface; (b) ice floats on water

13. Correct answers include ice melting, the decomposition of calcium carbonate (limestone or chalk) calcium oxide and carbon dioxide, the combustion of solid fuels, the decomposition of mercuric oxide to give oxygen and mercury metal and the decomposition of sodium nitrate into sodium nitrite and oxygen.

14. 36.9°

15. (a) hydrochloric acid; (b) water; (c) hydrochloric acid

16. Temporary hardness: dissolved calcium hydrogencarbonate; Permanent hardness: dissolved calcium sulphate.

17. When two elements combine with each other to form more than one compound, the weights of one element that combine with a fixed weight of the other are in a ratio of small whole numbers.

18. (a) magnesium, potassium, sodium, or calcium; (b) sodium or calcium; (c) magnesium; (d) magnesium; (e) carbon, sulphur; (f) chlorine

19. (a) copper sulphate, sodium carbonate, calcium sulphate; (b) ammonium dichromate; (c) calcium nitrate

20. (i) NH_4NO_3; (ii) Ammonium nitrate

21. (a) calcium carbonate, $CaCO_3$; (b) sodium carbonate Na_2CO_3; (c) iron, Fe (II) sulphate, $FeSO_4$; (d) calcium hydroxide, $Ca(OH)_2$

22. chlorine; fluorine; trihalomethanes (THMs); Salts of arsenic, radium, aluminium, copper lead, mercury, cadmium, barium

23. (a) any of methane, ethane, propane, butane; (b) any of pentane, hexane, heptane, octane, nonane, decane

24. (a) graphite; (b) lead oxide; (c) lead carbonate; (d) lead (II) oxide

25. Correct answers include silver, aluminum, zinc, nickel, iron, and platinum

26. (i) sand and a binder such as lime or gypsum; (ii) thermal decomposition

27. The upward buoyant force that is exerted on a body immersed in a fluid, whether fully or partially submerged, is equal to the weight of the fluid that the body displaces.

28. The amount of heat released during the combustion of a specified amount of it.

29. The temperature to which air must be cooled to become saturated with water vapor.

30. A watt is a unit of power, equivalent to one joule per second, which corresponds to the rate of consumption of energy in an electric circuit where the potential difference is one volt and the current one ampere.

31. (i) tungsten; (ii) nichrome; (iii) copper

ANSWERS: GENERAL INTELLIGENCE

TEST I

1. (a) Nephew; (b) Aunt; (c) Grandfather; (d) Grandmother; (e) Daughter-in-law

2. Booked an order to clean Mrs. Smith's chimney.
   Called at Mrs. Smith's house.
   Brushed the chimney.
   Looked to see if brush was showing from chimney.
   Cleared up any mess on the floor.
   Was paid by Mrs. Smith.

3. (a) 27; (b) 40; (c) 82

4. (a) quickly, slowly; (b) right, wrong; (c) seven, seventh; (d) toe, toes; (e) stable, horse; (f) animal, giraffe

5. (a) TOMATOES

6. STRUM

7. (c) they may be twins

8.

FARMER	GROCER	TAILOR
sty	pickles	twine
byre	jams	cotton
orchard	tea	scissors
trough	soap	tape measure

9. WAR; FATHER; ITALY; COMMAND; REGIMENT; SOLDIER; CAUGHT; OFFICER.

10.
(a) 3 + 5 + 11 = 19
(b) 4 x 4 + 2 = 18
(c) 7 x 12 ÷ 7 = 12 or 7 + 12 − 7 = 12
(d) 10 ÷ 2 - 2 = 3
(e) 6 - 10 + 6 = 2

11. WHITE: flour, salt, snow; RED: pillar box, ruby, lipstick; GREEN: emerald, grass, peas; BLACK: coal, soot, tar; YELLOW: banana, daffodil, mustard

12. 10 times.

13. 12

14. 4 times.

15. (a) 8.55 a.m.; (b) 8.20 a.m.

16. (a) 43; (b) 35; (c) 53; (d) 31; (e) 21

17. high; highly; hill; hilt; him; hinder; hinge; middle word: hilt

18. CANTERBURY

19.

    1. ROSE – E   2. TULIP - P   3. CROCUS - S
    4. PANSY -Y   5. LILY - Y   6. ASTER - R   7. DAHLIA - A
    8. VIOLET – T 9. ANEMONE – E   10. DAISY – Y

20. (a) PARTS; VSUDX (b) MONDAY

21. 1. wanted; 2. because; 3. ill; 4. teacher; 5. another;
    6. accompany; 7. his; 8. On; 9. and; 10. terrible

22. (a) 15; (b) twice; (c) 8; (d) ½; (e) 48; (f) 64,320; (g) 1

23. MERRY (or MARRY); STRENGTH; WRONG; TULIP;
    HEART; FLASK; LAUGH; SPRY

24. (a) Janet; (b) Mary; (c) Jane; (d) Jane *and* Janet

25. (a) F; (b) S; (c) P; (d) Y; (e) W; (f) S

26. (a) 12; (b) The missing number is either 3 or 19; (c) 17

27. (a) Anne; (b) Betty; (c) 6 years

28. (a) The groom put the *other* ten ponies into their stables.; (b) These difficult experiments were conducted by keen scientists; (c) We looked at our *blackened* faces bin the glass; we were not surprised that Ponting did not recognise us.; (d) The Essex is a *modern* make of typewriter.

29. (a) Mother; (b) Grandson; (c) Brother; (d) Niece

30. accept, refuse; glove, hand; carpenter, saw; dwell, live; good, better; colour, brown; they, them.

EXAM 2

1. CAREFULLY & IT

2. number

3. thrush, cow & bee; bus, bicycle, plane

4. (a) 5, 6, 7; (b) 2, 1; (c) 32, 64; (d) 1, 3, 3 ½; (e) 5, 50, 5,000

5. Smith

6. Be careful, we are watched.

7. (a) umbrella; (b) wood; (c) meat; (d) bread; (e) sweeper; (f) bicycle; (g) petal; (h) smoke; (i) polish; (j) theatre; (k) lemonade; (l) lesson; (m) mustard; (n) bad; (o) idling

8. (a) Fred went into the town on his bicycle.

(b) The people cheered as the soldiers marched down the street.

(c) Tibby the cat caught a mouse.

(d) The children were running on the beach.

(e) Jane fell over the stool as she ran round the room.

(f) All the children stood still when the whistle blew.

(g) There are two boys and three girls in the family.

(h) Soldiers wear khaki clothes and airmen wear blue clothes.

(i) Jane made her way slowly over the cobbled road.

(j) The black horses dragged a load of corn to the barn.

(k) John played in the park.

(l) The people were so tired that they were glad to get a cup of tea.

(m) The kettle was boiling merrily on the hob.

(n) Katie was playing with her doll.

9. (a) house; (b) calm; (c) bad; (d) water; (e) arrow; (f) jail; (g) feet; (h) carving

10. The first to follow Jack across the brook was the farmer's younger daughter. My brothers all went to work at the same time.

11. (a) O; (b) S; (c) N; (d) O; (e) S; (f) N

12. (a) Susan; (b) Fred; (c) One cannot tell

13. Martha

14. (a) 4 miles; (b) north

15. (a) feet; (b) shed; (c) pen & brush; (d) air

16. (a) 6; (b) x, x, (multiply); (c) 15; (d) x, +, −

17. (a) night; (b) plant; (c) bed; (d) stocking; (e) rough; (f) small

18. (a) telescopes; (b) a burial place; (c) a tool; (d) a score at football; (e) a fish

ANSWERS: VERBAL REASONING

1. (a) (E) CHAT WEARS; (b) (I) PANT BRAIN; (c) (R) FIST PRAWN; (d) (H) CLOT SHORT; (e) (P) SORT PLACES; (f) (P) TRAM PIPER.

2. (a) (WAY) ALWAYS; (b) (RAN) ARRANGED; (c) (NUT) MINUTE; (d) (TIN) PAINTING; (e) (LOW) GLOWING; (f) (LIP) SLIPPERS.

3. (a). 26; (b). 16; (c). 7; (d). 7; (e). 3; (f). 10

4. (a) tread, step; (b) smooth, ease; (c) manual, handbook; (d) lone, single; (e) diminish, decrease; (f) rotate, revolve.

5. (a) STEAM: The coding method is to step forwards by 1 space, then 2 spaces etc.; (b) GMUCJN: Step forwards 1 space, backwards 2, forwards 3 etc.; (c) CHAIRS: Step back one space; (d) VPNLF: Step back one space, then two, then one, then two etc.; (e) TASTE: Step forward five spaces; (f) DBNEBOT: Step one forward then three forward then repeat.

6. D

7. 4

8. (a) February, June; (b) liquid, solid; (c) tea, coffee; (d) sailor, soldier; (e) string, skin; (f) rise, sing.

9. (a) 86745; (b) 38455637; (c) TALLEST.

10. (a) 214531; (b) TREAD; (c) PARADE.

11. a) Formerly the girl was a help to her mother, now she is a hindrance.

b) Although the exterior of the building looked ugly, the interior was quite attractive.

c) Metals expand when heated, but contract when cooled.

d) The entrance to the cinema is very wide, but the interior/exit is rather narrow.

e) The hero was proud in the hour of victory, but the vanquished were ashamed in the hour of defeat.

f) Wealth makes a man lazy, but poverty makes him industrious/hardworking.

g) My friend's pearls are real and expensive, not fake and cheap.

h) This evening, in the darkness, I lost my watch, but tomorrow, in daylight I hope to find it.

i) The young and the hopeful should remember the old and the fearful/pessimistic.

j) The Scriptures teach us to love truth and hate lies.

12. a) I called to him, "Stay where you are."

b) Gareth asked his teacher, "Can I have a new pencil?"

c) Mary replied, "I will be going home tonight."

d) The boy was told, "You and your friends should return tomorrow."

13. a) DISTURB Hooligans caused a disturbance in the High Street.

b) BRUTE The brigands made a brutal attack on the travellers.

c) PERMISSION 'Permit me to accompany you, Sir,' said Mr. Micawber.

d) AGREE There was agreement among us not to touch each other's property.

e) INSTRUCT We were given our instructions and then dismissed.

f) DEMONSTRATION The conjuror prepared to demonstrate how the trick was done.

g) ORIGIN One must enter only original poems in the competition.

h) MAJESTY The great liner sailed majestically down the channel.

i) COWARD Long John Silver was guilty of many crimes but cowardice was not one of them.

j) BREVITY The chairman made a brief speech and sat down.

ACKNOWLEDGEMENTS

Grateful thanks go to the management and staff of the marvellous Institute of Education for scouring their amazing archives to find exam papers from the end of the war to the nineteen-sixties. It's wonderful that such material, and much more, is available for scrutiny by interested parties.

Also, we are deeply thankful for the astonishing knowledge and patience with us mere mortals of Hugh Barker, who provided answers where there were none. We knew that if Hugh could not come up with an answer, there was definitely something wrong with the question!

Thanks also to the examiners down through the decades who strove to come up with questions that were fair and equitable and that chimed with what students in a multitude of schools were being taught. Their exam boards, too, are deserving of praise and thanks for the great work they did and still do.

Robert Nichols of Palazzo Editions provided much-needed encouragement and patience during the compilation of *Are You Smarter Than a Baby Boomer?* and *Are You Smarter Than a Millennial?* for which I am very grateful.